Federal Donuts

MIKE SOLOMONOV
STEVEN COOK

TOM HENNEMAN ○ BOB LOGUE ○ FELICIA D'AMBROSIO

PRODUCED BY DOROTHY KALINS INK
PHOTOGRAPHS BY MICHAEL PERSICO
DESIGN BY DON MORRIS DESIGN

A RUX MARTIN BOOK
HOUGHTON MIFFLIN HARCOURT
BOSTON NEW YORK 2017

For information about permission to reproduce selections
from this book, write to Permissions, Houghton Mifflin Harcourt
Publishing Company, 3 Park Avenue, 19th Floor, New York,
New York 10016.

www.hmhco.com

Library of Congress Cataloging-in-Publication Data is available.

ISBN 978-0-544-96904-9 (hardcover); 978-0-544-96859-2
(ebook)

Printed in China
TOP 10 9 8 7 6 5 4 3 2 1

*Sally Levitt Steinberg tells us in *The Donut Book* (Storey
Publishing, 2004) that her grandfather, Adolph Levitt, who
invented the donut machine in the 1920s, found the
Optimist's Creed in a dime-store frame and adopted it.

FedNuts Kids
from left: Leo Henneman,
Leo Cook, Danny Cook,
Eva Cook, and David
Solomonov

"AS YOU RAMBLE THROUGH LIFE, BROTHER,
WHATEVER BE YOUR GOAL,
KEEP YOUR EYE UPON THE DOUGHNUT,
AND NOT UPON THE HOLE."
—THE OPTIMIST'S CREED*

WHAT'S INSIDE...

MIKE SOLOMONOV

JAMES BEARD AWARD-
WINNING CHEF OF ZAHAV
AND COFOUNDER OF
COOKNSOLO RESTAURANTS.
RESPONSIBLE FOR ALL IDEAS
INVOLVING CHICKEN SUITS.

STEVEN COOK

FORMER BANKER AND CHEF,
AND COFOUNDER OF
COOKNSOLO RESTAURANTS
(ZAHAV, ABE FISHER,
DIZENGOFF). CURRENTLY
LOOKING FOR HIS NEXT CAREER
(IF YOU HEAR OF ANYTHING).

TOM HENNEMAN
NARROWLY ESCAPED A CAREER IN COMMERCIAL REAL ESTATE, GREW A BEARD, AND REEMERGED AS FEDNUTS' MANAGING PARTNER.

BOBBY LOGUE
OWNER OF BODHI COFFEE SHOPS. CONVINCED FOUR OTHERS THAT A NASTY, GREASY PIZZA PARLOR COULD BE THE START OF AN EMPIRE. BOB BUILT THE ORIGINAL STORE WITH HIS OWN HANDS.

FELICIA D'AMBROSIO
YOUNGEST AND COOLEST FEDNUTS PARTNER. RESPONSIBLE FOR HASHTAGS, F-BOMBS, HAND SIGNALS, DANCE MOVES, AND SOCIAL MEDIA.

INTRODUCTION

"MMM, DOUGHNUTS. IS THERE ANYTHING THEY CAN'T DO?" —HOMER SIMPSON

WE GET ASKED ALL THE TIME "WHY CHICKEN AND DONUTS?" IT'S A FAIR QUESTION. PERHAPS IT'S *THE* QUESTION. AND IT'S OFTEN DELIVERED IN A TONE SUGGESTING WE MAY NOT HAVE BEEN IN OUR RIGHT MINDS.

Perhaps we meant to do chicken and waffles, but got disoriented—like how Columbus thought he had reached Asia, or Neil Armstrong thought he'd landed on the moon. But there's a more fundamental question: Why donuts at all?

Thinking of donuts instantly puts me back in high school football practice on Saturdays. If we'd won our game the night before, the practice would be short and joyful, a far cry from summer two-a-days. The coaches worked hard to be stern and serious as we heroically recounted our bumps and bruises. Soon released into the crisp Michigan autumn, with thirty-six hours to kill before the next practice, we would pile into a friend's beat-up AMC Eagle station wagon and head straight for the Franklin Cider Mill, leaving with grease-stained paper bags of hot cider donuts. We'd spend the rest of the afternoon watching college football on TV. Those were our salad days, and donuts were the salad.

Virtually every culture has a dessert of sweetened fried dough—proof of the donut's universal appeal. But donuts occupy a special place in America—we eat about 10 billion of them a year—and the donut shop is a particularly American institution. Perhaps it has something to do with the ingenuity that surrounded the rise of the donut in this country. In 1920, Adolph Levitt, an immigrant fleeing czarist Russia, developed the first automatic donut machine, churning out eighty dozen identical donuts an hour for Broadway theater crowds. This encouraged fledgling chains like Krispy Kreme and Open Kettle (later called Dunkin' Donuts) to spread the gospel of automatic donut machines (and their donut progeny).

Famed tourist attraction in La Puente, CA.

THE DONUT HOLE

~IT'S THE QUALITY~

And in both World Wars, volunteer "Donut Dolls" went overseas to boost morale, giving donuts to American troops. For a time, Ellis Island immigrants were met by the Salvation Army with a blanket and a donut—literally their first taste of America. But above all is our blessed American belief in egalitarianism. At a nickel apiece, donuts were an affordable luxury even during the Great Depression, establishing the donut's enduring image as the food of the everyman: the cop on the beat, the construction worker on the job site, the office worker at her desk.

Every morning, Federal Donuts has the privilege of helping people start their day. A donut and a cup of coffee may be small things, but that and a smile can be more than enough. Tom remembers a lesson from his father: You never know who you're talking to—you don't know where they've come from or what kind of day (or life) they've had.

Federal Donuts began as an idea to inject fun and meaning into our professional lives. We found that meaning in getting to know the people who come into our shops every day. Now, Federal Donuts is a successful business and a respected brand. But most important, it's a community: of five partners who didn't know each other that well when we began this journey; of our tremendous staff who have taken our vision further than we ever imagined; and of the guests who share a bit of themselves with us each day. Donuts changed our lives. And this book is a love letter to them, the people who make them, and the people who eat them. —*STEVEN COOK*

CHAPTER ONE

ACCIDENTAL ENTREPRENEURS: THE FEDNUTS ORIGIN STORY

"THERE WAS NEVER A MOMENT EARLY ON WHEN ANY OF US SAID NO. IT WAS JUST LIKE EACH IDEA THAT WAS INTRODUCED WAS OKAY: DONUTS, YES. CHICKEN, YES. COFFEE, YES. NAME, YES."
—BOBBY LOGUE

ON THE SLIPPERY SLOPE

BOBBY: We were hanging out on 2nd Street outside my coffee shop and a restaurant Mike and Steve owned then, and Mike asked what I was up to. And I said, "I'm going down to look at this greasy pizza parlor." And he was like, "Let's go."

STEVE: I was like, "No fucking way." So Mike went down without me and came back and said, "You've gotta see this."

BOBBY: I remember calling Mike a few weeks later, after he came home from Israel, and he said, "I've got a lot of things going on. I really don't know if we're gonna be able to do anything right now." And I said, "We wanna do donuts." And he said, "I'll call you right back!" And literally the next morning we all sat down to breakfast.

TOM: We wanted a meeting and Mike said, "Hey, let's go out to Café Soho. They make great Korean fried chicken." And we were out there eating, and Mike was like, "There's no place like this in Center City." And that's how it turned into "What if we did donuts for breakfast and chicken for lunch?"

WE KNEW NOTHING ABOUT MAKING DONUTS

STEVE: Once we settled on donuts, I was like, "How do you make donuts?" I remember Googling "donut machine."

MIKE: We got a hand hopper, which is essentially a pancake batter dispenser, and we were just doing that over the fryer.

STEVE: And that's when you became obsessed with the idea of the Donut Robot.

MIKE: Yeah, I wanted that Robot.

STEVE: Then we decided to do cake donuts. That was our first decision.

MIKE: We wanted it to be small, low-tech. And for yeast donuts, you need a lot of space and . . .

FELICIA: Pastry chefs.

MIKE: Pastry chefs can be really temperamental. And we loved the hot cake donuts from Brown's in Ocean City. 'Cause that was also something that nobody was doing then. Fresh, hot donuts.

BOBBY: Do you remember the day we went up to Sanders Supply?

STEVE: Oh my God. Sanders Supply. Yeah, that was terrifying.

The little shop on 2nd Street is just around the corner from Federal Street, and now you know the origin of FedNuts' name.

One day the Donut Robots may rise up and overthrow us.

TOM: So there's this massive five-story warehouse on 5th Street, north of Allegheny Avenue, on the railroad tracks.

BOBBY: Something about it was just, like, postapocalyptic. You went in, and each floor was the size of half a football field, just full of scrap metal and the occasional piece of restaurant equipment. And you had to climb over things and dig through to see what was there, you know?

MIKE: I remember walking by an elevator shaft and thinking, *Note to self, don't go by that*. And I walked down a flight of steps and I guess it was—who's the guy?

STEVE: Lew.

MIKE: And Lew says, "You don't wanna go down there." I'm like, "Are there zombies down there? Are there dog fights?"

BOBBY: And that was where we sourced 90 percent of our equipment for the opening.

WE MEET THE DONUT ROBOT

BOBBY: Then we drove to Harrisburg to buy a used Donut Robot. We met the guy in a Wendy's parking lot.

MIKE: I wanna say like a KFC . . .

STEVE: It was a national chain.

MIKE: It was a national chain, but I don't think it was quite as nice as Wendy's. It might have been Wendy's.

FELICIA: Roy Rogers?

MIKE: Yeah, that's what I was gonna say.

BOBBY: And the backstory on the original Belshaw Donut Robot was that the seller had used it only on Sundays at his church.

TOM: But that was it.

MIKE: 'Cause I feel like if it was Wendy's, I would've gotten something to eat. And it took us like seven hours to drive back.

"ONCE WE HAD SETTLED ON DONUTS, I WAS LIKE, HOW DO YOU MAKE DONUTS? I REMEMBER GOOGLING 'DONUT MACHINE.'"
—STEVE COOK

DEVELOPING THE RECIPE

MIKE: And then we tested donuts in the basement of one of our restaurants. No ventilation for the first couple months. I remember we had a couple people come in, too, like press people, to try the donuts.

STEVE: We weren't ready. We were totally not ready.

MIKE: That's when we were filling them.

"THE KEY WAS TO TAKE A PERFECTLY GOOD DONUT AND JAM A BUNCH OF FUCKING HOLES IN IT. AND THEN FILL IT WITH CUSTARD OR SOMETHING."
— MIKE SOLOMONOV

STEVE: With a custard that would, over time, be absorbed into the donut. So you'd fill a donut at 8 a.m. and someone would open it up at 11 a.m. and there'd be nothing inside. And they took forever to make.

MIKE: It took us a while to nail the batter. The donuts kept coming out bad.

STEVE: I remember trial after trial after trial, we made the batter and the donuts were just like bread—it was like eating white bread.

MIKE: And then we said, "Well, we're making cake donuts. Let's just take cake batter and fry that." And that sucked. It was the densest thing ever.

STEVE: And finally we said, "Let's just add 10 percent more butter and sugar."

MIKE: And that tasted pretty good. "Let's add even more butter and sugar."

BOBBY: Twice! We've changed the master recipe twice since we opened. Kept making it more fattening each time—that's the key.

NAH, WE'LL BE FINE

STEVE: Right before the opening, I remember thinking, *I just threw away a $7,000 investment and I'm okay with that.* The original sales model was, maybe we can do $7,000 a week. That would have been enough to just barely keep it going.

MIKE: We thought we'd need three employees throughout the day, and it would

only take one person to make all the donuts and chicken.

STEVE: You were like, "Anybody can make donuts." We didn't know what to expect. In the runup to the opening, there was a lot of anticipation, but the comments sections of the local blogs were filled with haters.

TOM: "Who's gonna go to Pennsport?"

BOBBY: Yeah. "Fried chicken and donuts?"

FELICIA: "Nobody will ever go there."

STEVE: I remember discussing the week before we opened how many chickens we should order, because we needed them two days in advance for the cure. I think we started with thirty-five orders.

From the Department of the Obvious: More butter and more sugar make donuts better.

"REMEMBER WE THOUGHT WE WOULDN'T NEED A DISHWASHER, THAT WE WOULD DO ALL THE DISHES OURSELVES?"
—FELICIA D'AMBROSIO

FELICIA: Oh my God, I remember talking to Mike and he's like, "How many chickens should we get?" And I'm like, "A million. As many chickens as we can do, as many as possible." And he was like, "Nah. We'll be fine . . ."

OPENING DAZE 10.16.11

STEVE: So we get in at 4 a.m. Two guys were making donuts. Mike and I jumped in. We were already behind.

BOBBY: I was still bolting stuff down.

TOM: He's blowing on paint.

STEVE: How fast did we sell out of "Fancies" that first day?

FELICIA: Immediately. They lasted less than an hour.

MIKE: We were in the fucking weeds. And our batter wasn't good. The donuts kept breaking in half on the flipper part of the Robot. And Steve had a slotted metal spoon and was trying to catch one to assist it flipping. And the donut broke. It was like all of life depended on that one donut.

STEVE: The board was filled with handwritten tickets—half dozen, dozen, dozen—and every donut you lost . . .

TOM: Was a two-minute setback.

FELICIA: And there was a line of fifty to seventy-five people waiting for chicken.

BOBBY: Out the door. I walked the line down the block and asked, "How many do *you* want? How many do *you* want? How many do *you* want?" And about halfway down the line, we were already out of chicken. I went back in and I said, "We're already sold out. Before we served our first piece. What are we gonna do?" And we were like, "Let's just give it away."

MIKE: But I remember, even when we started frying chickens, it was such a fucking nightmare. We were taking them out of the one fryer and putting them in the other for the second fry. There was no way to keep track of the count. We were all exhausted.

FELICIA: And doing dishes.

MIKE: Doing goddamned dishes.

STEVE: Washing greasy plastic containers in cold water.

MIKE: I remember telling jokes to people that were waiting in line and just being like, "Here's chicken! Please don't hate us."

BOBBY: We got a standing ovation from everybody when we said, "Chicken's free!" The whole line screamed and applauded.

"PEOPLE CAME IN AND ORDERED TWO DOZEN. WE'RE LIKE, 'ALL RIGHT, THAT'S ONE FIFTH OF EVERYTHING THAT WE HAVE.'"
—MIKE SOLOMONOV

DAY TWO: NOT MUCH BETTER

TOM: By day two we went out there thinking *We're gonna kill it.* An hour and a half later, we're in that same spot, like, "What the fuck just happened?"

"ONCE WE WERE RUNNING OUT OF DONUTS, WE WERE LIKE, 'WE GOTTA DO CHICKEN NOW,' 'CAUSE THERE WAS ALREADY A LINE OF PEOPLE."

—TOM HENNEMAN

FELICIA: It was like *Groundhog Day*. We didn't realize the limitation of having so little refrigeration space for chicken.

TOM: Or storage.

FELICIA: And the donut batter was so temperamental.

MIKE: Yeah. The donut is not an easy thing to make.

FELICIA: We started warming the batter with a hot-water bath as soon as it got cold out.

MIKE: And we started getting in really early, like midnight, just so we could get it all done.

TOM: We were basically a twenty-four-hour operation that was open for like three hours.

MIKE: Steve lived in the neighborhood anyway, so he would go in at 6 a.m., and then I would be fetching buttermilk at one in the morning. If you need to get buttermilk twenty-four hours a day, you go to Aramingo and then 5th, I believe.

FELICIA: The ShopRite? Pathmark?

MIKE: It was the Pathmark. They had so much buttermilk.

FELICIA: And on the third day, we realized we had to limit how much chicken you were allowed to buy, because people would come in and say, "I'm gonna take ten," and we said, "Oh, no, you can't do that. It's all we have." So we limited it to one whole chicken per person.

The wait for chicken on opening day. Behind the smiles, an angry mob is stirring.

TOM: We did that for a while.

FELICIA: We angered a lot of people.

STEVE: The biggest thing that hurt us was we were doing so much more volume than we even remotely expected.

MIKE: Having such a single-focus thing, nobody was really doing that. It was literally three items that were kind of related but not really. There were no side dishes. Our sides were a donut and pickles.

STEVE: We took a lot of shit, though, for running out. That was the big theme.

FELICIA: We still do.

TOM: People thought we did it on purpose.

FELICIA: Everybody said it was like a technique to drive business, the intentional shortage.

MIKE: After we got written up in the *New York Times,* we had all these random people driving forever to get here. There was a guy who came from Athens, Ohio, on a fucking

25

Greyhound bus just to show up to no food. I gave him a T-shirt.

TOM: That was a bummer. It definitely helped to create some of the initial buzz around the opening, but it was not something we were proud of.

A number guaranteed you access to chicken that day. Pretty soon, people started waiting in line just for the numbers.

AND THEN IT GOT COLD

TOM: And the weather started fucking with the donut batter.

STEVE: Yeah, and if you were working in the shop, your feet were freezing, because it was over an uninsulated basement.

TOM: The hood was sucking out the heat.

BOBBY: It was also pulling cold air in at the same time. And it was a cold winter.

STEVE: And then the finished donuts would sit there.

FELICIA: And get cold.

STEVEN: It'd be like sixty degrees in the shop, and the donuts weren't good.

BOBBY: And we couldn't keep the oil hot enough in the fryer.

MIKE: Didn't we put heat lamps on top of the fryer?

BOBBY: Yeah, and we got a big zipper cover thing for the donut rack, and we put space heaters underneath, too.

STEVE: It was like taking care of baby chicks. And it made the donuts, like, a little bit less bad.

TOM: I look back at pictures of those early donuts and I just cringe.

STEVE: For the first few years we were open, every donut was a crapshoot. Could be great—could suck.

THE SECOND STORE

STEVE: We were sort of expecting adulation, but we got hammered.

TOM: People expected us to open and not have any problems. And we had problems.

FELICIA: The original store was so unique and zany and neighborhood-y, but this customer was different. They reacted very differently to things. Even things that were okay, they would just be really harsh about.

STEVE: We weren't the underdogs anymore. We also got a little bit full of ourselves, and we were like, "We're gonna have a totally separate menu at the Center City store." So we opened with six brand-new "Fancies," totally different than in South Philly, three different Hot Fresh flavors, and three different chicken flavors.

TOM: We thought people would be like, "Oh, that's cool. You know, if you go to South Philly, you can get this." But then we realized that nobody cared except us.

"PEOPLE WERE GIVING US BUSINESS ADVICE. THEY WERE LIKE, 'I CAN'T BELIEVE THESE GUYS ARE SO STUPID. WHY DON'T THEY JUST MAKE MORE?'"
—STEVEN COOK

STEVE: Right, and nobody wanted a green tea donut.

TOM: They didn't.

MIKE: No. Nobody wanted a green tea donut.

FABRIC OF PHILLY

MIKE: People tell us all the time, "You know, this experience I had was fantastic in this one shop at this hour." And I'm thinking to myself, *You bought like a fucking cup of coffee.* But they were obviously really touched by that person who served them that coffee or that donut, you know?

STEVE: I thought Federal was going to be the equivalent of a band doing, like, a little fun side project. You know? We'll release one album, but it'll never become anything.

We did our best to find the humor in our capacity limitations.

Every year FedNuts has the privilege of sponsoring a couple of Taney Baseball teams. These kids remind us why we do this in the first place.

Hopefully it'll make enough money that it'll just stay open.

MIKE: We'll never make a living from it!

TOM: Yet we've become a part of the fabric of the city. On the weekends now, we have people who are in Philly for the day who come because they've heard great things.

FELICIA: Donuts appeal to most people. There aren't too many people who are like, "I just hate donuts." We got a letter the other day from a guy with a picture of his kid having his first donut ever at Federal Donuts. People send us pictures from Japan and India and Bali, all of them wearing their Federal Donuts T-shirts and telling us about flying donuts to their out-of-town family or expat Philadelphians.

"SOMETIMES PEOPLE WILL BE LIKE, 'THE STAFF IS SO FUNNY, THEY'RE ALWAYS DANCING.' AND WE'RE LIKE, 'WELL, YEAH, BECAUSE WE'RE SO NERVOUS AND YOU WON'T STOP STARING AT US.'"
—FELICIA D'AMBROSIO

MIKE: For a business that's only a few years old, I mean, the cult following is really remarkable. And also being embraced by the city—it would be a lot easier for them to just hate on us.

STEVE: I think it's the whimsical nature of it. I don't think you can describe Federal Donuts to people without them being like,

"Oh my God!" Just the idea of it makes people happy. And then it turns out to be better than it had to be.

BOBBY: Yeah. I think each one of us loves Philadelphia and loves the fact that we've made a little contribution. My favorite thing is just standing out on a Saturday morning and watching a half dozen kids come in with their parents and just smile. The kids are so excited to be there. So that alone is enough. Even if the business failed, it would have been enough that thousands of kids came through here and had a blast. You know?

FedNuts sells donuts and chicken at Citizen's Bank Park, the home of the Philadelphia Phillies.

MY NAME IS DR42

I'M A DONUT ROBOT. I'M ALSO THE SIXTH FOUNDER OF FEDERAL DONUTS. YOU WON'T READ ABOUT ME IN THOSE SANITIZED FEDNUTS HISTORIES. THE ONLY REASON THEY INCLUDED MY STORY HERE IS BECAUSE CONTROVERSY SELLS BOOKS.

I was there in the beginning, working out of an unventilated basement, riffing on donuts as fast as we could think of them. I made all the donuts that first year. You know, the year *The New York* freaking *Times* called our donuts "world class."

Where am I now? Locked up in the basement below one of the stores. Tom and Felicia sometimes stop by to say hi, but I can tell how uncomfortable it makes them. They called me a hunk of junk, but I seem to remember another hunk of junk that made the Kessel Run in less than twelve parsecs. It's called the *Millennium Falcon.* Ever hear of it?

So they replaced me, just like that. We had a taste of success and, all of a sudden, I was an embarrassment. I guess when you're going corporate, raw donuts aren't punk anymore.

The new guy's name is Mark (Donut Robot Mark II, to be precise), and he's just as you'd imagine him: perfectly boring. They said Mark could adjust his frying cycle—no more raw donuts. Big deal; what's rock and roll about that? Sure, his donuts are perfectly round and plump, but can he name every Metallica album in the order they were released?

I didn't ask to make history. For most of my life I performed once a week on Sundays in a church parking lot. They'd tear open a bag of powdered donut mix, add water, and let me do my thing. The kids couldn't get enough of me.

Then one day, they put me in a van and drove me to a Wendy's parking lot outside of Harrisburg, Pennsylvania. That's where I first met Bobby and Mike and Steve. They seemed like cool guys at the time, and besides, my solo act wasn't going anywhere and I wasn't getting any younger.

They bring me back to their shop and ask me to show them what I can do. Only these idiots can't figure out how to put me together. They're trying to reinstall my arm—the one that flips the donuts in the oil once they're halfway cooked— only they put it in completely backward. They turn me on and there's this horrible noise—metal on metal, just terrible—and they're laughing. I mean, imagine someone forcing your arm to rotate in a way it doesn't want to go and laughing. It fucking hurts.

So that's pretty much how they treated me, at least until they met that corporate robot Mark and had no more use for me. They're saving me for when FedNuts is so huge, there'll be like a FedNuts museum, where people can see the Donut Robot that launched a thousand donut stores. Yeah, right. But if it does happen, they better fucking give me my cut.

You think this is FUN? Does it look like fun to you? Well, maybe the coating in Strawberry Sugar part.

CHAPTER THREE

MAKING DONUTS AT HOME

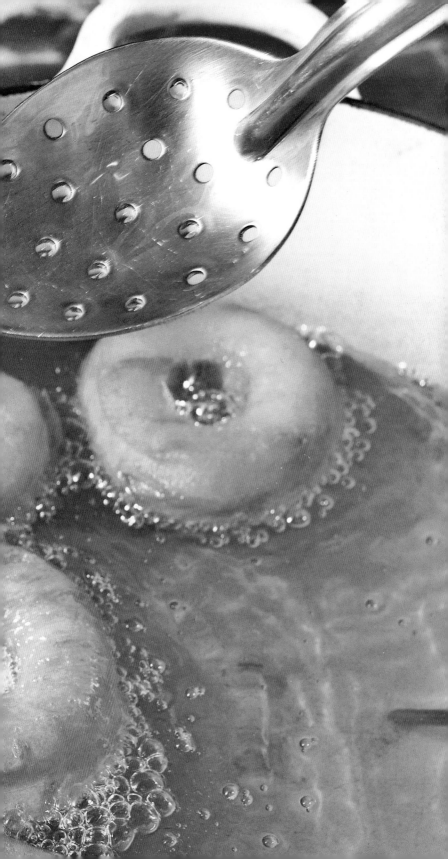

WHEREIN WE ASK YOU TO FRY THINGS

CAN'T DONUTS BE BAKED, YOU MIGHT ASK? WELL, TECHNICALLY, YES. BAKED DONUTS ARE A THING, BUT SO IS PUTTING BANANAS IN FRUIT SALAD, AND YOU DON'T SEE ANYONE WRITING A BOOK ABOUT THAT.

Besides, fried foods are one of the great glories of the universe. French fries. Donuts. Need we say more? No other cooking method can achieve such a perfect state of duality within a single morsel of food—crispy on the outside, moist and tender within. Some things are even fried twice (see page 144).

And lest you think that fried foods are reserved for state fairs and restaurant kitchens, there are big rewards for frying at home. At Federal, we clean our oil through filters woven from angels' wings, but our competitors may not be as scrupulous. There's nothing worse than food fried in old, spent oil. At home, you're in control. And it's badass to deep-fry at home. Your friends and neighbors will find you more attractive, and your children will think you are a golden god. So break out the Dutch oven, throw open the window, and let's get frying!

WHAT ABOUT THAT FRYING OIL?

You can reuse frying oil a few times (fried chicken, anyone?), as long as you filter it between uses. For best results, pour the oil through a fine-mesh strainer lined with a coffee filter or paper towels into a clean jar. Cool the oil to room temperature before handling. Store it in the fridge or freezer until your next frying session.

Afterward, just throw away the jar of oil. Some cities have sites that accept used oil to be converted into biofuel. Or find a neighborhood restaurant that will accept your oil in their used-oil bin.

MEET MATTHEW FEIN

Matt Fein was a line cook at Zahav in 2012 when we ruined his career by tapping him to help open our second FedNuts store as the "Fancy Maker," our highest-skilled and most demanding position, with responsibility for lining the shelves with six different donut beauties by 7 a.m. each day. Three months later, Matt took over from our opening chef and has overseen the growth of a complex operation that includes four permanent stores, two seasonal locations, and more to come.

Matt is the chief creative officer of Federal Donuts. If you've ever taken a bite of a "Fancy" donut and your eyes rolled back in your head, you have him to thank. His first invention was the French Toast donut, one of the most beloved FedNuts of all time. His favorite creation is the Chocolate Éclair (page 103), based on the Good Humor bars of his youth. But no one's perfect: Matt was also responsible for the short-lived Watermelon Cucumber Lime donut.

DONUT DOUGH IN 12 STEPS

E'VE NEVER BELIEVED THAT RECIPES SHOULD BE CLOSELY GUARDED. FOOD IS FOR SHARING, AND A RECIPE IS WORTHLESS WITHOUT GOOD EXECUTION. BUT THIS IS AS CLOSE AS WE'VE COME TO A TRUE TRADE SECRET. WE'VE IMPROVED OUR **MASTER DONUT RECIPE** (PAGE 58) THREE TIMES SINCE WE OPENED IN 2011, AND WE ARE PLEASED TO SHARE IT WITH YOU. SHOULD YOU WANT TO USE IT TO OPEN YOUR OWN DONUT SHOP, GOOD LUCK WITH THAT!

1. The dough starts with a modest amount of flour; additional flour will be incorporated in the rolling process.

2. Baharat (kalustyans.com) is the secret ingredient in our batter. Think of it as a sweet and savory Middle Eastern "pumpkin pie" spice.

3. Salt keeps the donuts from tasting flat. We use fine sea salt, but table salt is good, too. Baking soda and baking powder make them light and fluffy.

4. Blend the dry ingredients thoroughly to avoid overmixing the batter when the wet ingredients are added.

 5. We use only egg yolks for richness and texture.

6. Beat the yolks and sugar together until they thicken, turn pale yellow, and the paddle or beater leaves trails in the mixture.

TIP:
Ingredients go into the bowl of a stand mixer, though you can certainly use a hand mixer, or even a sturdy whisk.

7. Weighing ingredients is nice, but not crucial. We have added more sugar to our recipe over the years for more tender donuts, but the batter is not overly sweet.

8. Stream in the melted butter slowly so it can emulsify with the egg mixture.

9. Add the buttermilk and mix briefly until it is incorporated.

10. The dry ingredients go in all at once and are mixed until just incorporated. Pause to scrape down the sides of the bowl midway through mixing.

11. The finished batter will be soft and sticky, and thicker than a traditional cake batter.

12. Scrape the batter out onto a very well-floured piece of parchment paper.

49

ROLLING THE DOUGH

PREPARE A WORK SPACE WITH A LARGE PIECE OF PARCHMENT PAPER FASTENED AT THE CORNERS WITH TAPE. HAVE 1 CUP OF FLOUR IN A BOWL NEARBY TO USE AS NEEDED. GENEROUSLY FLOUR THE WORK SURFACE.

1. The donut batter is sticky, so keep a thin layer of flour between the dough and your hands.

Don't be shy: Flour your hands, flour the rolling pin— when in doubt, flour it!

2. Roll out the dough until it's about ½ inch thick.

3. With well-floured hands, gently shape the dough into a rough rectangle still about ½ inch thick.

CUTTING THE DONUTS

*D*ONUT HOLES DON'T EXIST JUST TO PLEASE CHILDREN. WITHOUT A HOLE IN THE CENTER, DONUTS (ESPECIALLY CAKE DONUTS) FRY UNEVENLY, RESULTING IN EITHER AN UNDERCOOKED CENTER OR AN OVERCOOKED EXTERIOR.

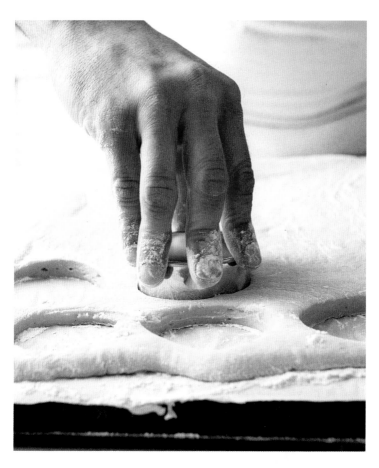

1. To make our donut shapes, we use two sizes of ring cutters, the larger about 2¾ inches in diameter. To make the holes, use a 1-inch cutter.

2. The advantage of rolling out donut dough is that you get the donut holes for free.

3. After cutting, carefully remove the excess dough. It can be rerolled, but it's even easier to cut it into small irregular pieces and fry as is.

4. Brush off any excess flour, then pop the donuts in the freezer for up to 30 minutes to make them easier to handle.

5. Gently lift the dough rings with a spatula to help preserve their shape during frying.

FRYING THE DONUTS

WE LIKE TO USE A BIG ENAMELED CAST-IRON POT BECAUSE IT RETAINS HEAT WELL AND HELPS MAINTAIN A CONSTANT OIL TEMPERATURE. OIL EXPANDS AS IT HEATS, SO DON'T FILL YOUR POT MORE THAN HALFWAY OR YOU WILL HAVE A MESS ON YOUR HANDS.

1. Clip a candy or deep-frying thermometer to the side of the pot and add 2 to 3 inches of canola or peanut oil. Heat on medium-low until the oil registers 375°F.

2. Carefully slide the dough rings into the oil with the spatula. Fry for about 90 seconds, or until the edges turn golden brown.

DONUT HOLES NEED ONLY 60 TO 90 SECONDS TO FRY AND OFTEN FLIP OVER BY THEMSELVES.

3. Flip the donuts and fry for another 90 seconds. Transfer the donuts to a rack set over a paper towel–lined baking sheet to drain. Toss with sugar, or cool briefly before glazing.

OUR MASTER DONUT RECIPE

SEE THE STEP-BY-STEP PHOTOS ON PAGES 44 TO 57. HAVE GLAZES AND SUGAR MIXTURES READY BEFORE FRYING: HOT DONUTS GO STRAIGHT INTO SUGAR MIXES. LET DONUTS COOL FOR UP TO 20 MINUTES BEFORE GLAZING.

- 12 large egg yolks
- 1 cup granulated sugar
- 5 tablespoons (2½ ounces) butter, melted and cooled
- 1¼ cups buttermilk
- 3½ cups all-purpose flour, plus 1 cup for rolling and cutting dough

- 1½ teapoons salt
- 1 teaspoon baking soda
- ½ teaspoon baking powder
- ¼ teaspoon baharat (kalustyans.com)

- Canola or peanut oil, for frying

MAKING THE DOUGH

1. Combine the egg yolks and sugar in the bowl of a stand mixer fitted with the paddle attachment. You can certainly use a hand mixer, or even a sturdy whisk, instead.

2. Mix on low speed until ribbons start to form in the mixture and the color lightens, about 3 minutes. Slowly stream in the melted butter until just incorporated, about 30 seconds.

3. Add the buttermilk all at once. Mix again just to combine, about 5 seconds.

4. In a separate bowl, whisk together the 3½ cups flour, salt, baking soda, baking powder, and baharat. Add to the mixer all at once and mix on low speed until incorporated, about 30 seconds. Scrape down the sides of the bowl and mix again on medium-low until the dough looks smooth and starts to pull away from sides of the bowl, 20 to 30 seconds.

ROLLING THE DOUGH

5. Prepare a counter work space by fastening a large piece of parchment paper with tape at the corners. Have the 1 cup of flour nearby to use as needed. Generously flour the work surface.

THIS RECIPE MAKES 12 TO 18 DONUTS, PLUS DONUT HOLES.

6. Scrape down the paddle attachment and turn all the batter out onto the floured surface. Dust the top of the dough with more flour, sprinkling the edges as well. Flour your hands well, too.

7. With a floured rolling pin, roll out the dough to a ½-inch-thick rectangle, about 10 by 14½ inches. Add more flour to prevent sticking. Brush the excess flour off the dough and parchment paper with a pastry brush. Transfer the dough on the paper to the back of a baking sheet and slide it into the freezer for up to 30 minutes.

CUTTING THE DONUTS

8. We use two sizes of ring cutters to make our donut shapes: the larger about 2¾ inches in diameter, and a 1-inch cutter for the holes. (Feel free to use a drinking glass and a shot glass.) Flour the cutters well and often to prevent sticking. Begin with the large cutter, then cut out the smaller holes. Return the baking sheet with the dough rings to the freezer until ready to fry. (At this point, the frozen rings can be wrapped in plastic and stored in the freezer for up to 2 days. Let thaw slightly before frying.)

9. The dough scraps can be gathered together and rerolled, or cut into small, irregular shapes and fried as they are.

FRYING THE DONUTS

10. Clip a candy or deep-frying thermometer onto one side of a big enameled cast-iron pot and add 2 to 3 inches canola or peanut oil. Heat over medium-low until the oil reaches 375°F.

11. Carefully lift the dough rings with a spatula and slide them into the oil, about 4 at a time, depending on the size of your pot. After about 90 seconds, the edges will begin to brown; flip the donuts with a slotted spoon. Fry for another 90 seconds until golden brown and delightfully puffy. (Donut holes take 60 to 90 seconds and tend to flip themselves.) With a slotted spoon, transfer the donuts on a rack set over a paper towel–lined baking sheet to drain. Reheat the oil to 375°F before cooking the next batch.

12. Toss the hot donuts in one of the Hot Fresh Sugar Mixes (pages 60 to 71), or let the donuts cool and then glaze (pages 72 to 113).

*T*HE ONLY THING BETTER THAN TOSSING FRESHLY FRIED DONUTS IN FLAVORED SUGAR IS DOING IT WITH A FRIEND. THE HEAT OF THE DONUTS AWAKENS THE AROMATICS OF THE SUGAR, AND THE WARM, SOFT CAKE MELTS IN YOUR MOUTH.

BREAK OPEN A DONUT AND PRETEND TO STUDY THE INTERIOR CRUMB STRUCTURE. THEN SAY SOMETHING PROFOUND LIKE, "THE BATTER'S A TOUCH DENSE TODAY."

SUGAR CLINGS BEST TO DONUTS THAT ARE RIGHT OUT OF THE FRYER. BEFORE YOU START FRYING, MAKE SUGAR MIXTURES IN LARGE BOWLS. THEN DROP THE HOT DONUTS INTO THE BOWLS AND GET IN THERE WITH YOUR FINGERS TO MIX EVENLY AND COAT WELL.

VANILLA SPICE

1 cup granulated sugar

1 vanilla bean, split lengthwise, seeds scraped with the tip of a knife

¼ teaspoon freshly grated nutmeg

¼ teaspoon ground coriander

⅛ teaspoon salt

Mix all the ingredients together in a large bowl. Use a fork or a wooden spoon to break up and distribute the vanilla seeds in the sugar. Toss the hot donuts in the sugar mixture with your fingertips and turn to coat well.

Hot Fresh Sugar Kids:
Sally Cook, Annie Logue, and
Tessa Logue, foreground.

HOT FRESH SUGAR MIXES

CINNAMON BROWN SUGAR

1 cup granulated sugar

¼ cup light brown sugar

1½ tablespoons ground cinnamon

¼ teaspoon freshly grated nutmeg

⅛ teaspoon salt

Whisk all the ingredients together in a large bowl until combined, breaking up any clumps of brown sugar with a fork. Toss the hot donuts in the sugar mixture with your fingertips and turn to coat well.

STRAWBERRY LAVENDER

1 cup granulated sugar

2 tablespoons Strawberry Nesquik or other strawberry-flavored powder

1 tablespoon ground freeze-dried strawberries

1 teaspoon ground lavender flowers

1/8 teaspoon salt

Whisk all the ingredients together in a large bowl. Toss the hot donuts in the sugar mix with your fingertips and turn to coat well.

FREEZE-DRIED STRAWBERRIES AND LAVENDER FLOWERS ARE READILY AVAILABLE ONLINE.

CHAPTER FIVE

GLAZED DONUT "FANCIES"

THREE STEPS TO GLAZING PERFECTION

> JUST REMEMBER: COOL DONUTS, WARM GLAZE.

1. Improvise a **DOUBLE BOILER** by adding about 2 inches of water to a saucepan and setting it over medium heat. Bring the water to a simmer.

2. Place a bowl of **GLAZE** over the saucepan and heat through. Use your fingertips to glaze each cooled donut (see **GLAZING 101**, page 76).

3. COOL the glazed donuts on a rack set over a paper towel–lined baking sheet until the glaze is dry, about 10 minutes.

BASIC MILK GLAZE

THIS IS THE SIMPLEST OF ALL TOPPINGS, BUT IT'S HARD TO BEAT. THE HUMBLE MILK GLAZE BRINGS INTO FOCUS THE PURE VIRTUES OF THE DONUT ITSELF.

3¾ cups confectioners' sugar	½ cup whole milk
	¼ teaspoon salt

Whisk all the ingredients together in a large bowl until smooth. Follow **THREE STEPS TO GLAZING PERFECTION**, above.

GLAZING 101:
IT'S ALL IN THE WRIST

GLAZING DONUTS IS ALL ABOUT ATTITUDE AND CONFIDENCE. A FEDNUTS ARTISAN CAN GLAZE A DOZEN DONUTS WITHOUT BREAKING EYE CONTACT WITH THE CUSTOMER. FOLLOW THESE STEPS AND NOW YOU CAN, TOO!

1. Hold the bottom of the donut with your fingertips and submerge the top in warm glaze a little more than halfway up the sides.

2. Remove the donut from the glaze and, with a twist of the wrist, turn it right side up, allowing the excess glaze to wrap around the sides and bottom of the donut.

3. Transfer the glazed donut to a wire rack and let the glaze set for about 10 minutes.

BLACK & WHITE

WE CREATED THIS DONUT AS A ROOSTER SOUP (PAGE 196) KICKSTARTER REWARD FOR OUR GOOD FRIEND AND REAL ESTATE GURU TIM DUFFY IN HONOR OF HIS DAUGHTER, QUINN. WE LOVE ITS UNCANNY RESEMBLANCE TO A BLACK AND WHITE COOKIE.

MILK GLAZE

- 3¾ cups confectioners' sugar
- ½ cup whole milk
- ¼ teaspoon salt

Whisk all the ingredients together in a large bowl until smooth. Follow *THREE STEPS TO GLAZING PERFECTION*, page 74.

DARK CHOCOLATE GLAZE

- ½ cup plus 1 tablespoon chopped bittersweet chocolate
- ¼ cup plus 1 tablespoon unsweetened cocoa powder
- ¼ teaspoon salt
- ½ cup whole milk
- 3 cups confectioners' sugar

Combine the chocolate, cocoa powder, salt, and milk in a large bowl. Set the bowl over a saucepan of simmering water over medium heat and whisk until the chocolate is melted. Add the confectioners' sugar and continue whisking until the mixture is smooth.

After the Milk-Glazed donut has cooled, dip half into the warm Dark Chocolate Glaze, following *GLAZING 101*, page 76.

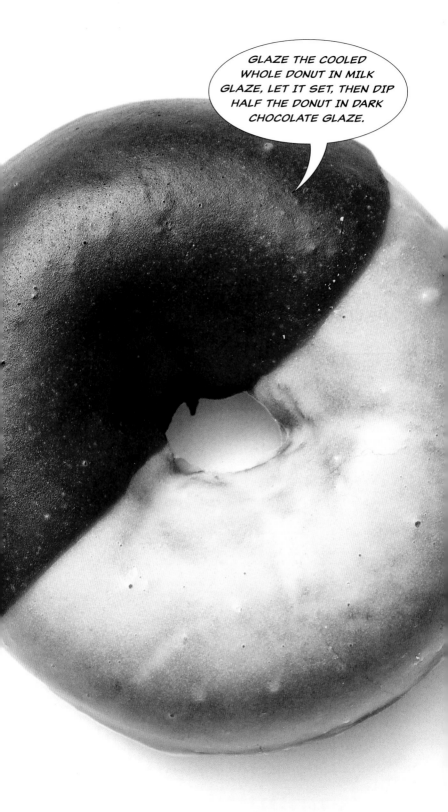

SALTED TEHINA GLAZE

PRESENTING THE SESAME BAGEL IN DONUT FORM. THE SAVORY QUALITY OF TEHINA (OR TAHINI, PURE SESAME PASTE) ENHANCED WITH A BIT OF SALT IS A GREAT FOIL FOR THE DONUTS' SWEETNESS. USE THE BEST-QUALITY TEHINA—WE USE SOOM, AN ARTISANAL PRODUCER AND OUR NEIGHBOR IN THE CITY OF BROTHERLY LOVE.

3¾ cups confectioners' sugar

½ cup tehina (tehini)

½ cup water

1 tablespoon salt

½ cup sesame seeds, toasted

Whisk all the ingredients together in a large bowl until smooth. Follow *THREE STEPS TO GLAZING PERFECTION*, page 74.

GRAPEFRUIT BRÛLÉE

THIS IS OUR VERSION OF A HEALTHY WAY TO START YOUR DAY! WE LOVE THE CRUNCHY TEXTURE AND COMPLEXITY THAT COMES FROM CARAMELIZING THE GLAZE, AND HOW THE SLIGHT BITTERNESS OF THE GRAPEFRUIT HARMONIZES WITH THE SUGAR.

GRAPEFRUIT GLAZE

- 3¾ cups confectioners' sugar
- ½ cup grapefruit juice
- 2 tablespoons finely grated grapefruit zest
- 1 tablespoon light corn syrup
- ¼ teaspoon salt

Whisk all the ingredients together in a large bowl until smooth. Follow **THREE STEPS TO GLAZING PERFECTION**, page 74.

BRÛLÉE TIP:
Hold a kitcthen torch 2 to 3 inches above the donut and steadily move it over the surface until the glaze melts, bubbles vigorously, and begins to brown. Stop a little short of your desired outcome—the sugar will continue cooking and darkening for a few seconds after the torch is removed. Or stick it under the broiler.

STRAWBERRY SHORTCAKE

ONUTS CAN BE ONE-DIMENSIONAL SUGAR BOMBS, SO WE LOVE THE WAY THOSE THAT INCORPORATE FRUIT EXPRESS BALANCE AND BRIGHTNESS. STOCK UP ON STRAWBERRIES WHEN THEY'RE AT THEIR PEAK, AND YOU CAN TASTE SUMMER ALL WINTER LONG.

VANILLA CREAM GLAZE

- 3¾ cups confectioners' sugar
- ¾ cup heavy cream
- 1 tablespoon plus 1 teaspoon vanilla extract
- ½ teaspoon salt

Whisk all the ingredients together in a large bowl until smooth. Follow *THREE STEPS TO GLAZING PERFECTION*, page 74, glazing the entire donut. Let cool.

STRAWBERRY GLAZE

- 1 pound strawberries, hulled and quartered
- ⅓ cup granulated sugar
- ½ teaspoon fresh lemon juice
- 1 tablespoon light corn syrup
- 1 drop red food coloring
- ¼ teaspoon salt
- 3½ cups confectioners' sugar

Make a strawberry puree by heating the strawberries and sugar in a medium saucepan over medium-low heat until juices are released and the fruit starts to break down, 5 to 7 minutes. Let cool. Transfer to a food processor and process until smooth. Place ½ cup of the puree in a large bowl, add all the other ingredients, and whisk until smooth.

Follow *THREE STEPS TO GLAZING PERFECTION*, page 74, with each Vanilla Cream–Glazed donut. Sprinkle on crumbs from an unglazed donut if you like.

MAKE CRUMBS BY TOSSING A LEFTOVER UNGLAZED DONUT INTO A FOOD PROCESSOR AND PULSING FOR A SECOND OR TWO.

BLUEBERRY MASCARPONE

THIS DONUT HAD PERHAPS THE LONGEST RUN OF ANY "FANCY" DONUT, AND WE CAUGHT HELL WHEN WE TOOK IT OFF THE MENU. THE RICHNESS OF THE MASCARPONE AND THE ACIDITY OF THE BLUEBERRIES WORK PERFECTLY TOGETHER, LIKE A SLICE OF BLUEBERRY CHEESECAKE.

MASCARPONE GLAZE

1 cup mascarpone cheese

¼ cup whole milk

¼ teaspoon salt

3¾ cups confectioners' sugar

Whisk the mascarpone cheese, milk, and salt together in a large bowl until smooth. Add the confectioners' sugar and continue whisking until combined. Follow *THREE STEPS TO GLAZING PERFECTION*, page 74. Let cool before drizzling.

BLUEBERRY DRIZZLE

1 pound blueberries	¼ teaspoon salt
⅓ cup granulated sugar	3½ cups confectioners' sugar
1 tablespoon light corn syrup	

Heat the blueberries and sugar in a small saucepan over medium-low heat until juices are released and the fruit begins to break down, 5 to 7 minutes. Transfer to a food processor and process until smooth. Strain if you like. Place ½ cup of the puree in a large bowl, whisk in the other ingredients, and follow the *DRIZZLING TIPS* on the next page.

DRIZZLING
TIP 1: There are no rules for decorating donuts, but using a whisk to drip a secondary glaze on top of a base glaze makes us feel like all that money our parents spent on art school wasn't wasted after all.

TIP 2:
Dip the business end of the whisk in slightly warm glaze, hold it about 4 inches above the donut, and drizzle away.

POMEGRANATE NUTELLA

HERE'S A REBOOT OF ONE OF OUR ORIGINAL FLAVORS, FROM BACK WHEN WE WERE FILLING EACH DONUT BY HAND. THIS VERSION MAKES THE SAME IRRESISTIBLE FLAVORS EVEN BETTER. GLAZE THE DONUT FIRST WITH POMEGRANATE, LET SET, THEN DRIZZLE ON THE NUTELLA.

POMEGRANATE GLAZE

- 3¾ cups confectioners' sugar
- ¼ cup plus 3 tablespoons pomegranate juice
- ¼ cup pomegranate molasses
- ¼ cup sesame seeds, lightly toasted
- ¼ teaspoon salt

Whisk all the ingredients together in a large bowl until smooth. Follow *THREE STEPS TO GLAZING PERFECTION*, page 74.

NUTELLA DRIZZLE

- 3¾ cups confectioners' sugar
- ½ cup plus 1 tablespoon Nutella
- ¼ cup plus 2 tablespoons water
- ¼ teaspoon salt

Whisk all the ingredients together in a large bowl until smooth. Drizzle the warm Nutella onto the Pomegranate-Glazed donut using the *DRIZZLING TIPS* on page 90.

S'MORES

S'MORES

MARSHMALLOWS ARE A GREAT BASE FOR A DONUT GLAZE. TOASTED IN THE OVEN AND COMBINED WITH DARK CHOCOLATE AND GRAHAM CRACKER CRUMBS, THEY MAKE THIS DONUT TASTE LIKE ITS NAMESAKE.

MARSHMALLOW GLAZE

- 1 (1-pound) bag marshmallows
- ½ cup water
- ¼ teaspoon salt
- 3¾ cups confectioners' sugar

Preheat the oven to 400°F. Place the marshmallows on a baking sheet lined with parchment paper and roast until browned, about 5 minutes. While they are still hot, mix the marshmallows with the water and salt, then add the confectioners' sugar.

GRAHAM CRACKER CRUMBS

- 2½ cups graham cracker pieces (about 16 squares)
- 2 sticks (8 ounces) unsalted butter, melted
- ¾ teaspoon salt

Grind the graham crackers in a food processor into fine crumbs, or crush with a rolling pin. Pour into a bowl; add the melted butter and salt. Mix well.

DARK CHOCOLATE DRIZZLE

- ½ cup plus 1 tablespoon chopped dark chocolate
- ¼ cup plus 1 tablespoon unsweetened cocoa powder
- ¼ teaspoon salt
- ½ cup whole milk
- 3 cups confectioners' sugar

Combine the chocolate, cocoa powder, salt, and milk in a large bowl. Set the bowl over a saucepan of simmering water over medium heat. Whisk until the chocolate is melted and the mixture is smooth. Add the confectioners' sugar and whisk until combined.

To assemble: Dip the cooled donuts in the Marshmallow Glaze, following **THREE STEPS TO GLAZING PERFECTION**, page 74. Apply the Dark Chocolate Drizzle using the **DRIZZLING TIPS** on page 90. Sprinkle with the Graham Cracker Crumbs.

CHOCOLATE PEANUT BUTTER

DURING THE 1970S, THE COMBINATION OF CHOCOLATE AND PEANUT BUTTER WAS ACCIDENTALLY DISCOVERED DURING THE FILMING OF A TELEVISION COMMERCIAL. WE WERE SO INSPIRED, WE CREATED THIS DONUT.

CHOCOLATE PEANUT BUTTER GLAZE

½ cup chopped bittersweet chocolate

¼ cup creamy peanut butter

½ cup plus 2 tablespoons milk

1 teaspoon salt

3¾ cups confectioners' sugar

Combine the chocolate, peanut butter, milk, and salt in a large bowl. Set the bowl over a saucepan of simmering water over medium heat. Whisk until the chocolate is melted. Add the confectioners' sugar and whisk until combined. Follow *THREE STEPS TO GLAZING PERFECTION*, page 74.

PEANUT BUTTER DRIZZLE

½ cup plus 1 tablespoon creamy peanut butter	¾ teaspoon salt
¼ cup plus 1 tablespoon water	3¾ cups confectioners' sugar

Combine the peanut butter, water, and salt in a large bowl. Set the bowl over a saucepan of simmering water over medium heat. Whisk until the peanut butter is melted, then add the confectioners' sugar and whisk until combined. Using the *DRIZZLING TIPS* on page 90, drizzle over the Chocolate Peanut Butter–Glazed donut.

CHOCOLATE ÉCLAIR
WITH ÉCLAIR CRUMBS

CHOCOLATE ÉCLAIR

NAMED FOR THE NOVELTY ICE CREAM BAR—NOT THE FRENCH PASTRY—THIS RECIPE USES OUR CHOCOLATE CAKE BATTER. IT'S THE SAME PROCESS AS OUR MASTER DONUT RECIPE, PAGE 58, BUT USES COCOA POWDER INSTEAD OF BAHARAT. THIS RECIPE IS A MAJOR BREAKTHROUGH FOR US. THOUGH MORE THAN ONE FEDNUTS PARTNER CONSIDERS OUR MILK GLAZE (PAGE 74) ON A CHOCOLATE DONUT TO BE THE PLATONIC IDEAL.

CHOCOLATE CAKE DONUT BATTER

3¼ cups all-purpose flour

¾ cup Dutch cocoa powder

1¼ cups granulated sugar

1½ teaspoons salt

1 teaspoon baking soda

¾ teaspoon baking powder

1½ cups buttermilk

1 stick (4 ounces) unsalted butter, melted

12 large egg yolks

Vanilla Cream Glaze, (page 84)

Whisk the flour with the cocoa powder in a large bowl, then follow the master recipe, page 58. Roll out and fry the donuts.

Let the donuts cool. Prepare the Vanilla Cream Glaze (page 84) and follow *THREE STEPS TO GLAZING PERFECTION*, page 74. While the glaze is still wet, toss each donut in the Éclair Crumbs until well coated.

ÉCLAIR CRUMBS

3 cups finely crushed Nilla Wafers

2 sticks (8 ounces) unsalted butter, melted

1 tablespoon salt

1½ tablespoons Dutch cocoa powder

Mix 2 cups of the Nilla Wafer crumbs, half the butter, and 1½ teaspoons of the salt in a large bowl until all the butter is absorbed by the crumbs.

Into a separate bowl, place the remaining wafer crumbs, remaining butter, remaining salt, and the cocoa powder and mix well. Let cool so the cocoa doesn't "bleed" into the white crumbs. Combine the contents of both bowls and mix well.

LEMON "MERINGUE" WITH LEMON GLAZE

THIS IS A SHOWSTOPPER WITH ITS EASY, SEXY MERINGUE—JUST FILL A PASTRY BAG (PREFERABLY FITTED WITH A STAR TIP) WITH MARSHMALLOW FLUFF AND PIPE IT ONTO THE LEMON-GLAZED DONUT. NOW ALL IT NEEDS FOR ITS STAR TURN IS A BRIEF RENDEZVOUS WITH A KITCHEN TORCH (OR A FEW SECONDS UNDER THE BROILER).

THE GLAZE
- 3¾ cups confectioners' sugar
- ½ cup fresh lemon juice
- 1 tablespoon light corn syrup
- ¼ teaspoon salt
- 1 tablespoon grated lemon zest

THE FILLING
- 2 cups Marshmallow Fluff

Whisk all the glaze ingredients together in a large bowl until smooth. Following **THREE STEPS TO GLAZING PERFECTION**, page 74, glaze the donuts and let cool.

Fill a pastry bag with the Marshmallow Fluff and pipe it generously into the center of each donut to make a pattern. (Optional: If you have donut holes or leftover donuts, use pieces to fill in holes before piping.) Use a kitchen torch to gently toast the Fluff. Or put the filled donuts on a baking sheet and place them under the broiler for 5 to 10 seconds, until the Fluff is lightly browned.

COOKIES AND CREAM

T HE COMBINATION OF CRUSHED OREOS AND VANILLA
CREAM GLAZE IS BOTH DEADLY SIMPLE AND
DEADLY DELICIOUS—LIKE DIPPING A COOKIE IN A
GLASS OF MILK.

Make the Vanilla Cream Glaze on page 84, adding ¼ cup finely crushed Oreos just before dipping the donut so the mixture doesn't turn gray. Follow **THREE STEPS TO GLAZING PERFECTION**, page 74. After the donuts are glazed but while the glaze is still wet, top with a sprinkling of crushed Oreos.

FRENCH TOAST GLAZE WITH CRUNCH AND MAPLE DRIZZLE

THIS ALL-TIME FAVORITE WAS ALSO THE STAR OF A CONCRETE OFFERED AT THE SHAKE SHACK LOCATED A FEW BLOCKS FROM OUR CENTER CITY SHOP.

FRENCH TOAST GLAZE

3¾ cups confectioners' sugar

1½ teaspoons ground cinnamon

½ teaspoon salt

½ cup heavy cream

2½ tablespoons vanilla extract

Whisk all the ingredients together in a large bowl until smooth. Follow **THREE STEPS TO GLAZING PERFECTION**, page 74.

FRENCH TOAST CRUNCH

12 ounces Cinnamon Toast Crunch cereal

1½ sticks (6 ounces) unsalted butter, melted

1 teaspoon salt

Crush the cereal into fine crumbs in a food processor or with a rolling pin. Add the melted butter and salt and mix well. Sprinkle over still-wet French Toast–Glazed donuts.

MAPLE DRIZZLE

3¾ cups confectioners' sugar

½ cup maple syrup

2 tablespoons water

½ teaspoon salt

Whisk all the ingredients together in a large bowl. Using **DRIZZLING TIPS** on page 90, drip Maple Drizzle over the French Toast Glaze and Crunch.

MILK AND COFFEE

COFFEE IS A SURPRISINGLY DIFFICULT FLAVOR TO CONVEY IN A DONUT. WE TRIED MANY FORMS OF COFFEE AND MANY METHODS OF FLAVOR EXTRACTION WITHOUT SUCCESS. ULTIMATELY, THE SIMPLEST SOLUTION PROVED BEST: DUSTING THE FRESHLY GLAZED DONUTS WITH FINELY GROUND HIGH-QUALITY COFFEE.

Make the Basic Milk Glaze on page 74, then follow *THREE STEPS TO GLAZING PERFECTION*, page 74. Sprinkle ¼ teaspoon (or more) finely ground coffee on each donut while the glaze is still wet.

DONUT YOU WANT A FEDNUTS WEDDING?

RINGS SYMBOLIZE NUPTIAL BLISS, SO IT WAS NOT SURPRISING THAT SOON AFTER WE OPENED FEDERAL DONUTS, COUPLES BEGAN REQUESTING TALL TOWERS OF DONUTS FOR THEIR WEDDING CAKES.

Sweetening up the big day means stacking fancy flavors onto multilevel tiered stands, creating the effect of a "cake" complete with floral embellishments and custom toppers, plus individually stickered bags to carry away take-home treats. No lifetime commitments are required: Donut towers have been deployed for birthdays, anniversary parties, corporate gigs, and other events, and require a minimum of nine dozen—and up to twenty dozen—donuts in four or five tiers that reach for the stars. *—FELICIA D'AMBROSIO*

CHAPTER SIX

FAN ART IN THE AGE OF FEDERAL DONUTS

DONUT CAN BE PRETTY TO LOOK AT, BUT IT'S NOT ART. FRIED CHICKEN CAN BE A CANVAS FOR BRUSHSTROKES OF SAUCE, BUT NO CURATOR WILL EVER HANG IT IN A MUSEUM. YOU CAN CREDIBLY ARGUE THAT ALL COOKING IS MORE CRAFT THAN ART, THOUGH CREATIVITY, DISCIPLINE, AND HAND SKILLS ARE EQUALLY REQUIRED.

WE WERE LUCKY TO START THIS BUSINESS IN PHILADELPHIA, WHERE STREET ART LIKE THOUGHT-PROVOKING TOYNBEE TILES, OUR OWN NOSEGO MURAL (COMMISSIONED FOR OUR 7TH STREET STORE, AND ON THE ENDPAPERS OF THIS BOOK), AND LEGAL GRAFFITI WALLS COEXIST WITH THE TOWERING PAINTINGS OF PHILADELPHIA'S FAMED MURAL ARTS PROGRAM, AND THE MAGNIFICENT COLLECTIONS OF THE BARNES FOUNDATION AND THE PHILADELPHIA MUSEUM OF ART.

YOU CAN'T HELP BUT BE INSPIRED HERE, AND SOMETIMES, YOUR OWN NOT-ART WORK CAN INSPIRE ACTUAL ARTISTS IN THEIR EXPRESSION. FUELED BY COFFEE AND FIRED UP ON DONUT GLAZE, THE ARTISTS ON THE FOLLOWING PAGES SHARED THEIR VISIONS OF FEDNUTS' PLACE IN THE UNIVERSE. WE ARE ETERNALLY GRATEFUL TO EVERYONE WHO MAKES PHILADELPHIA A MORE BEAUTIFUL PLACE TO BE. —FELICIA D'AMBROSIO

CINDY CHAN
The Federal Donuts Team
2016
Mixed media: acrylic, color pencils, digital

Federal Donuts

LORA MARIE DURR
Variety Fancy Box
2016
Oil on board

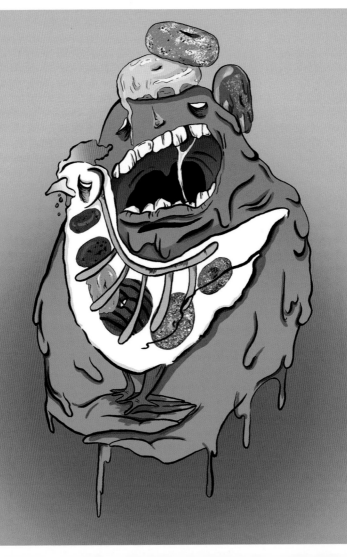

TIM BARNES

SYLVANA SAWIRES
Which Came First: The Chicken or the Donut?
2016
Acrylic on canvas

ALLISON CHANG
Rise N' Fednuts
2016
Washi tape, digital collage, watercolor, photograph

CHAPTER SEVEN

"WHY DON'T YOU MAKE MORE CHICKEN?"

ON INTENTIONAL SCARCITY

"THESE GUYS SHOULD REALLY CONSIDER CHANGING THEIR NAME TO 'FEDERAL YEAH, WE'RE OUT OF THAT.'"
—ONE-STAR YELP REVIEW, 11/27/2011

"I DON'T UNDERSTAND HOW 'THERE'S SIMPLY NO ROOM' IS ANY KIND OF EXCUSE FOR RUNNING OUT OF PRODUCT. GET A BIGGER FRIDGE, GET MORE DELIVER-IES THROUGH THE DAY, BUY YOUR NEIGHBORING BUILDING AND EXPAND, JUST DO SOMETHING!"
—FOOD BLOG COMMENT AFTER OUR FIRST STORE OPENING

The most ludicrous conversation we ever had at Federal Donuts took place before we even opened. It was October 14, 2011, three days before the planned opening of our first store. We gathered in the little Pennsport park that had become our de facto boardroom during construction.

The main purpose of this meeting was to determine how much chicken we needed for opening day. Since our fried chicken was a twenty-four-hour process, we had to decide right then how many chickens to order for the next day. Felicia was the only one who seemed to grasp that ordering too little might be a problem. The rest of us were worried about ordering too much. There was a real chance this wasn't going to be a profitable venture—the last thing we needed was to throw away leftover chicken.

What happened next has become part of FedNuts lore. We'd ordered enough chicken for about thirty servings, but we had a line twice that long before we even started selling it! So we decided to give it all away rather than disappoint so many people. If we had bottled the flop sweat on our brows at that moment, no one could ever accuse us of perpetrating intentional scarcity: the idea that we purposely limited supply to create the appearance of robust demand.

Frankly, we're not that smart. And even if we were, our bank account was running on fumes, and I doubt any of us would have had the balls to actively limit our revenues in exchange for some theoretical future payoff. The simple truth is that six hundred square feet only holds so many chickens. And when we opened our second store, it was also only 600 square feet. That really pissed people off. Now, in addition to being geniuses, we were also morons.

In 2013, we finally opened a commissary capable of producing enough chicken. And yet, to this day, we get asked if we still have chicken left, and people stay away on the assumption that we don't. If anything, the mirage of "intentional scarcity" has done more to hurt us than help us.

Federal Donuts is a business based on just three things—coffee, donuts, and fried chicken—and running it is a tightrope walk. If any one of those three things isn't great, there's nowhere to hide.

Our implicit contract with our guests is simple: We don't do many things, but we do those things well. So running out of chicken wasn't a hipster ploy to make us look cool, it was just making sure we lived up to our end of the bargain. But in a strange turn, it was an abundance of unused chicken parts that led us to our next restaurant adventure, Rooster Soup (page 196).

And damn—the chicken we did serve sure was good.

"WELL, IF YOU CAN ACTUALLY RUN IT LIKE A REAL BUSINESS AND HAVE PRODUCT ALL DAY LONG DURING YOUR POSTED HOURS OF OPERATION, IT MIGHT BE A GOOD ADDITION TO CENTER CITY. CURRENTLY, YOUR BUSINESS MODEL IN PENNSPORT HAS BEEN NOTHING SHORT OF A JOKE."

—FOOD BLOG COMMENT JUST PRIOR TO OPENING OUR SECOND STORE

CUTTING AND CURING TIPS

CUTTING UP WHOLE CHICKENS GIVES YOU THE BEST END PRODUCT—AND YOU GET THE BONES FOR FREE. WE BUILT A WHOLE NONPROFIT RESTAURANT, ROOSTER SOUP COMPANY, FROM FEDERAL DONUTS' CHICKEN BONES THAT WOULD OTHERWISE BE LANDFILL (SEE CHAPTER 9). BUT IF YOU ONLY LIKE DARK MEAT (OR WHITE), OR ARE JUST PLAIN LAZY, PRECUT CHICKEN WORKS FINE, TOO.

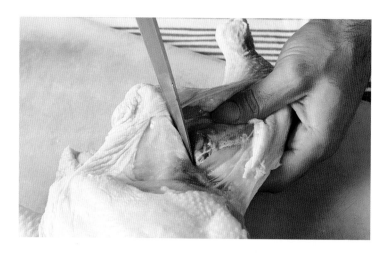

TIP 1: Curing the chicken overnight —essentially dry brining—helps keep the bird juicy and distributes the seasoning throughout the meat.

TIP 2: Onion and mustard powders provide sweet and savory accents to the chicken that keep you coming back for more.

TIP 3: Don't be afraid to get in there with your hands to make sure the seasonings are distributed evenly over the chicken.

TIP 4: Cure the chicken overnight in the refrigerator. The skin will dehydrate slightly, ensuring a crispier crust.

ALL ABOUT THE BATTER

A THIN BATTER GIVES KOREAN-STYLE FRIED CHICKEN ITS TRADEMARK CRUNCH. IT'S MORE CORNSTARCH THAN FLOUR BASED, WHICH RESULTS IN A DELICATE, CRISPY COATING THAT CRACKLES WHEN YOU SINK YOUR TEETH INTO IT.

1. Mix together the cornstarch, flour, and salt.

2. Slowly pour in the water and whisk until smooth and homogenous.

3. The finished batter should be relatively thin, like crepe or loose pancake batter.

4. Dunk the chicken pieces in the batter to coat and allow the excess to drip off before frying.

FRYING:
SO NICE WE DO IT TWICE

THE CHIEF DISTINGUISHING CHARACTERISTIC OF KOREAN FRIED CHICKEN VERSUS ITS COUSIN FROM THE AMERICAN SOUTH IS THAT IT'S FRIED TWICE: FIRST AT A LOWER TEMPERATURE TO COOK THE CHICKEN THROUGH AND THEN AT A HIGHER TEMPERATURE TO DEVELOP AN IRRESISTIBLE SHATTERINGLY CRISP CRUST.

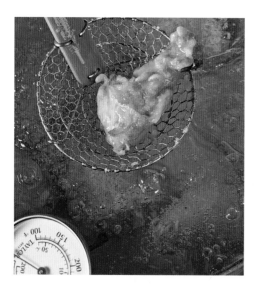

1. When the oil temperature reaches 300°F, add the legs and thighs.

2. After about 3 minutes, add the breasts so that the white and dark meat will each be cooked for the right amount of time.

3. Drain the chicken on paper towels and allow to rest while the oil reaches the right temperature for the second fry.

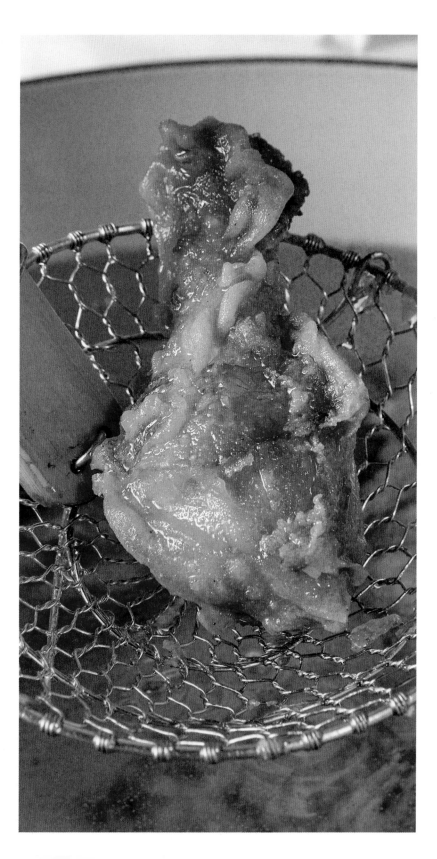

Fried Chicken Friends:
Tessa Logue and Eva Cook

MASTER FRIED CHICKEN RECIPE

FRIED CHICKEN WAITS FOR NO ONE, SO HAVE YOUR SPICE BLENDS AND GLAZES READY BEFORE YOU START FRYING. SEASON THE CHICKEN IMMEDIATELY AFTER IT'S FRIED. OUR PROCESS BEGINS WITH CURING THE CHICKEN OVERNIGHT, OR AT LEAST 4 HOURS AHEAD, AND THEN FRYING IT TWICE FOR AN EXTRA-CRISPY CRUST. ONLY THEN DO WE TOSS THE HOT FRIED CHICKEN INTO A SPICE BLEND OR BRUSH ON A TASTY GLAZE.

THE CURE

- 1½ tablespoons salt
- 4 teaspoons onion powder
- 2 teaspoons dry mustard

THE CHICKEN

- 1 whole chicken (about 4 pounds), cut into 10 pieces (including wings)

THE BATTER

- 3 cups cornstarch
- 1½ cups all-purpose flour
- 2 teaspoons salt
- 3 cups cold water

- 2-3 quarts canola oil, for frying

THE CURE

1. Combine all the cure ingredients in a large bowl and mix until well blended. Add the chicken parts and get in there with your hands to coat each piece well.

2. Put the coated pieces of chicken on a baking pan and cover with parchment paper or plastic wrap. Refrigerate for at least 4 hours, or overnight.

THE BATTER

3. Combine the cornstarch, flour, and salt in a large bowl and mix well. Slowly pour in the water and whisk until the mixture is smooth and the consistency of thin pancake batter.

MAKES 10 PIECES.

TWICE-FRIED CHICKEN

CLIP A CANDY OR DEEP-FRYING THERMOMETER ONTO ONE
SIDE OF A BIG ENAMELED CAST-IRON POT AND ADD 2 TO
3 QUARTS OF CANOLA OIL, ENOUGH SO THE CHICKEN PARTS
WILL BE FULLY SUBMERGED. OIL EXPANDS AS IT HEATS, SO
DON'T OVERFILL THE POT.

4. Heat the oil over low heat until it reaches 300°F. Meanwhile,
bring the cured chicken to room temperature—you don't want to
fry ice-cold chicken because it throws off the timing. When the oil
is hot, dip each chicken piece into the batter to fully coat.

5. Hold a corner of each piece with your fingers and slide the
battered legs and thighs into the oil. Be careful not to splash the
hot oil! After 1 minute, add the wings; after 3 minutes, the breasts.

6. Use a spoon to make sure the chicken pieces don't stick
together or to the bottom of the pot. If they do stick, gently
separate them with the spoon, without tearing the precious crust.

7. After 10 minutes total, with a slotted spoon, remove the
chicken pieces to drain on paper towels. (The chicken won't be
fully cooked—there's a second fry.)

8. Let the chicken rest for 15 to 20 minutes. While it hangs out,
reheat the oil to 350°F. Fry the chicken pieces again, this time for
4 minutes, or until golden brown and crispy.

9. With the slotted spoon, remove the chicken pieces to drain on
a rack set over a fresh paper towel–lined baking sheet. If using a
spice blend, drop the hot chicken pieces right into the bowl with
the spices and dust to coat. If using a glaze, use a paint brush or a
silicone brush to spread on the hot glaze.

SPICE BLENDS FOR
TWICE-FRIED CHICKEN

ZA'ATAR SPICE BLEND

LONG BEFORE FEDERAL DONUTS, WE TESTED FRIED CHICKEN RECIPES IN THE ZAHAV KITCHEN. WE ALWAYS ENVISIONED GLAZING THE CHICKEN THE WAY OUR FAVORITE KOREAN FRIED CHICKEN JOINTS DID, BUT WE HAD NEVER CONSIDERED DRY SEASONINGS. ONE DAY, AS WE PULLED A BATCH OF CHICKEN FROM THE FRYER, A JAR OF ZA'ATAR, THAT MIDDLE EASTERN SPICE BLEND OF WILD HERBS AND SUMAC, WAS SITTING THERE TAUNTING US. WE REACHED FOR IT AND A MENU ITEM WAS BORN.

1 cup za'atar	½ cup sumac

Combine all the ingredients in a large bowl and mix well. In the same bowl, dust the hot twice-fried chicken with the spice blend.

COCONUT CURRY SPICE BLEND

OUR FAVORITE THAI CURRY SOUPS, ENRICHED WITH COCONUT MILK, INSPIRED THIS BLEND. THE SWEETNESS OF THE COCONUT, THE SAVORY, FRAGRANT SPICES, AND A TOUCH OF CHILE HEAT CONSPIRE TO CHALLENGE AND SATISFY AT THE SAME TIME.

- 1 cup sweetened coconut flakes, toasted in a 350°F oven on a baking pan
- 1 cup Madras yellow curry powder
- ¼ cup sumac
- 1½ tablespoons ground cinnamon
- 1 tablespoon salt
- 1 tablespoon granulated sugar
- 1 tablespoon ground ginger
- 1 tablespoon onion powder
- 1 tablespoon cayenne pepper

Combine all the ingredients in a large bowl and mix well. In the same bowl, dust the hot twice-fried chicken with the spice blend.

BUTTERMILK RANCH SPICE BLEND

THERE'S NOTHING SOPHISTICATED ABOUT THIS SEASONING BLEND—WE USE IT STRAIGHT OUT OF THE PACKAGE. RANCH IS ONE OF THE GREAT FLAVOR DISCOVERIES IN AMERICAN HISTORY, AND THIS IS FEDNUTS' MOST POPULAR CHICKEN SEASONING.

> 1 (2-ounce) packet
> ranch salad dressing
> and seasoning mix

Put the seasoning in a large bowl and dust the hot twice-fried chicken with the spice blend.

BALLPARK BARBECUE SPICE BLEND

AS SOON AS THE FIRST FEDNUTS SHOP TOOK OFF, BOBBY SET HIS SIGHTS ON GETTING US A BALLPARK STAND AT CITIZENS BANK PARK, HOME OF THE PHILADELPHIA PHILLIES. WE CREATED THIS SPECIAL CHICKEN SEASONING TO CELEBRATE OUR FIRST SEASON THERE.

¼ cup light brown sugar

¼ cup sumac

2 tablespoons smoked paprika

2 tablespoons salt

1 tablespoon onion powder

1 tablespoon dark chili powder

1 teaspoon dried thyme

1 teaspoon freshly ground black pepper

Preheat oven to 350°F. Combine all ingredients in a bowl and mix well. Line a baking pan with parchment paper and spread the spice mixture evenly on the pan. Bake for 10 to 15 minutes, until the mixture is fragrant and maroon in color. Let cool. Grind in a food processor until fine. Pour it onto the hot twice-fried chicken from a seasoning shaker, or sprinkle it on the chicken with your fingers.

GLAZES FOR
TWICE-FRIED CHICKEN

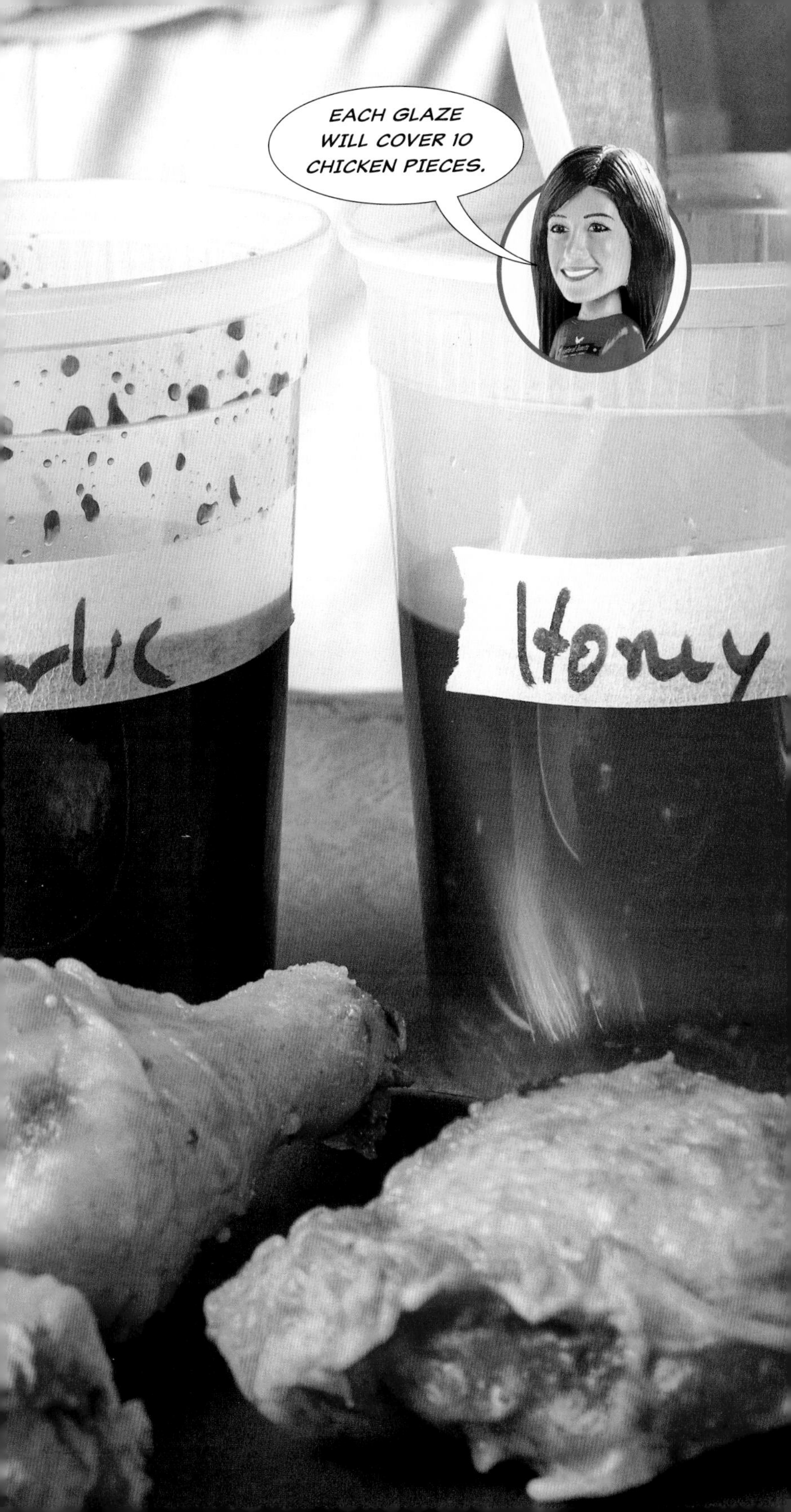
EACH GLAZE WILL COVER 10 CHICKEN PIECES.
Honey

CHILI GARLIC GLAZE

YOUR BRAIN SAYS "NO" BUT YOUR MOUTH SAYS "YES." FORTUNATELY, THERE'S JUST ENOUGH SWEETNESS IN THIS SPICY GLAZE TO KEEP IT FROM ACTUALLY BLOWING YOUR HEAD OFF.

- ¼ cup granulated sugar
- 2 tablespoons cayenne pepper
- ¼ cup cold water
- 1 cup chili garlic sauce (store-bought)

- ½ cup sherry vinegar
- ¼ cup white soy sauce (Japanese shoyu)

Combine the sugar, cayenne, and water in a large bowl and whisk until the sugar has dissolved. Add the remaining ingredients and continue whisking until smooth. Use a large paintbrush to coat the hot twice-fried chicken with glaze.

SOY GARLIC GLAZE

THIS IS OUR HOMAGE TO THE SOY GLAZE AT THE INIMITABLE CAFÉ SOHO IN NORTH PHILADELPHIA, WHOSE UTTERLY ADDICTIVE KOREAN FRIED CHICKEN WINGS WERE A MAJOR SOURCE OF INSPIRATION FOR US. WITHOUT CAFÉ SOHO, FEDERAL DONUTS MIGHT JUST BE A DONUT SHOP.

- 1 large head of garlic
  Olive oil for drizzling
- 1 cup kecap manis (store-bought sweet, thick soy sauce)

- ¼ cup sherry vinegar
- ⅓ cup white soy sauce (Japanese shoyu)
- 1 tablespoon red pepper flakes

Preheat the oven to 350°F. Cut off the top of the garlic to expose the cloves. Drizzle with oil and wrap the entire head in foil to seal. Roast for 55 minutes until golden brown and the cloves are tender. Let cool, then squeeze the cloves out into a large bowl. Add the remaining ingredients and mix well. Use a large paintbrush to coat the hot twice-fried chicken with glaze.

HONEY GINGER GLAZE

THIS GLAZE BRINGS THE SWEET WITHOUT THE HEAT. SHERRY VINEGAR AND A HEALTHY DOSE OF FRESH GRATED GINGER KEEP IT FROM BEING CLOYING. IT ALSO CURES THE COMMON COLD.

1 cup honey
3/4 cup sherry vinegar

1/3 cup plus 1 tablespoon white soy sauce (Japanese shoyu)
1/4 cup grated peeled fresh ginger

Combine the honey, sherry vinegar, and soy sauce in a large bowl and mix until smooth, then mix in the ginger. Use a large paintbrush to coat the hot twice-fried chicken with glaze.

FRIED CHICKEN SANDWICH

WE CREATED THIS SIMPLE BUT INCREDIBLY DELICIOUS SANDWICH FOR A POP-UP SUMMER LOCATION, AND IT WAS SUCH A HIT THAT WE DECIDED TO ADD IT TO OUR MENU PERMANENTLY—THE ONLY NEW ITEM WE'VE EVER INTRODUCED. NOW IT'S OUR SINGLE BEST-SELLER! IT'S WORTH SEEKING OUT MARTIN'S POTATO ROLLS—THEY'RE THAT GOOD.

1 tablespoon onion powder

1 teaspoon dry mustard

1½ teaspoons salt

4 (4-ounce) boneless, skinless chicken breasts

2 quarts canola oil, for frying

4 Martin's Potato Rolls

4 slices American cheese

1 cup dill pickle chips

1 packet ranch salad dressing and seasoning mix

½ cup Spicy Rooster Sauce (opposite)

1. Combine the onion powder, mustard, and salt in a small bowl. Put the chicken breasts in a larger bowl, pour the spice mixture over them, and toss until all the pieces are thoroughly coated. Refrigerate until ready to cook (only a few hours!).

2. Make the Chicken Batter (page 148) and batter the chicken.

3. Heat the oil to 300°F in a large enameled cast-iron pot fitted with a candy or deep-frying thermometer, following the procedure on page 144. Fry for 3 minutes. Remove the chicken breasts from the oil and cool on a rack set over paper towels for 10 minutes.

4. For the second fry, reheat the oil to 350°F, fry the chicken for 3 minutes more, and drain well on paper towels.

5. Split the potato rolls. Put 1 slice of cheese on each roll top and melt under the broiler. Put 4 to 5 pickle chips on each bottom roll. Sprinkle ranch dressing mix over the fried chicken breasts, coating well. Then put a chicken breast on each bottom bun. Drizzle Spicy Rooster Sauce over the chicken and top with the melted cheese roll.

SPICY ROOSTER SAUCE

Whisk together ½ cup mayonnaise and 2 tablespoons hot sauce
(we love Frank's RedHot) in a bowl. Add a pinch of cayenne pepper
and continue whisking until the sauce is smooth and creamy.
Makes enough for 4 sandwiches.

CHAPTER EIGHT

DONUTS THAT ARE BETTER THAN OURS

WE'VE FRIED ENOUGH BAD DONUTS IN OUR DAY TO KNOW THAT IT ISN'T AS EASY AS IT LOOKS. SO WHEN WE FIND A DONUT IN THE WILD THAT MAKES US CLOSE OUR EYES, SMILE, AND FEEL AT ONE WITH THE WORLD, YOU KNOW WE'RE GOING TO WANT TO SHARE.

A fresh batch of donuts ready to be packed up at Blue Star Donuts in Portland, OR.

BROWN'S

ST. CHARLES AND BOARDWALK, OCEAN CITY, NJ
BROWNSOCNJ.COM

WHEN YOU'RE IN YOUR TWENTIES, WORKING NIGHTS AND LINE-COOKING EIGHTY HOURS A WEEK, WAKING UP AT 5 A.M. IS ABOUT AS APPEALING AS FALLING DOWN A STEEP FLIGHT OF STAIRS.

So when a coworker asked me to go surfing with him one morning fifteen years ago, it was the last thing I wanted to do. But I said yes anyway. On the agreed-upon morning, I slithered out of bed and into a Volkswagen that ferried us to the boardwalk in Ocean City. As the sun rose and I began to sober up, I immediately began to make excuses for why we should go back to Philly: **1.** Tsunamis **2.** Sharks **3.** Tsunamis in shark-infested waters **4.** I can't swim very well **5.** I want to sleep **6.** I really fucking hate you right now. "Dude. Brah. You're gonna love it," said my friend. And in the same breath: "Dude. Brah. We can get hot donuts from Brown's afterward!"

Okay. For hot donuts, I could suffer through frigid water and tsunamis and sharks. And I did, paddling hard and going nowhere, slamming face-first into a dense sandbar and swallowing enough salt water to brine my internal organs. Finally and at last, I was released from my surfing obligation. As I crawled onto the beach through the dirty sand, exhausted and delirious, I gazed across the crowded boardwalk and saw a line forming. I could smell vanilla and honey and all things good and holy wafting from a little window next to a cafe.

We got in line and slowly inched toward that window. Soon we were within sight of the donut machine. I became hypnotized watching the batter automatically drop from the hopper, fraying slightly at the edges when it met the hot oil. The donuts continued along, conveyed and flipped by the machine before magically rising out of the bubbling fat to drain. Then, a final dunk in honey. And before I knew it, it was our turn. **—MIKE SOLOMONOV**

Doesn't get better than Brown's hot donuts in the summer sun.

DYNAMO DONUT + COFFEE

2760 24TH STREET AND
110 YACHT ROAD, SAN FRANCISCO, CA
DYNAMODONUT.COM

IT'S NOT TOO MUCH OF A STRETCH TO SAY THAT WITHOUT DYNAMO DONUTS, THERE MIGHT NOT BE A FEDERAL DONUTS. THE SUMMER AFTER BOBBY AND I OPENED BODHI COFFEE, I FLEW TO SAN FRANCISCO TO VISIT FRIENDS AND CATCH A BREATHER FROM THE SHOP.

Before opening Bodhi in 2010, I'd been recently laid off. I wasn't getting any younger, and after bouncing around jobs in commercial real estate and logistics, I was beginning to feel lost and anxious. I never would have considered opening a coffee shop if Bobby hadn't approached me, but now, behind the counter, things just made sense. We weren't making a ton of money, but the feeling of helping people start their day and the sense of community that came with it—there's nothing better.

So I was feeling a certain kind of way when I arrived in San Francisco. The first morning, we headed down to the Mission District to check out Dynamo Donuts, which my friends had raved about. The place hadn't opened yet when we arrived, but a line had

Maya Henneman meets the Maple Glazed Bacon Apple.

already formed. As we neared the front, I heard a customer ask for a blueberry donut. "Sorry," replied the cashier. "We didn't get fresh blueberries in today." *Whoa,* I remember thinking. *This place puts fresh fruit in their donuts?!*

We ordered at the outdoor counter and made our way to the indoor seating area, where we passed a cook picking fresh herbs for a donut glaze. The place was bustling with neighborhood types and tourists, and the haze of freshly ground coffee enveloped the room in a way that made it feel like the only place to be.

I don't remember everything we ate except that it was all delicious, including the much-raved-about Maple Bacon donut. Today, maple bacon is standard issue for new-wave donut shops, but back then, at the beginning of the artisanal donut boom, it felt fresh and exciting. As we left, I had only two thoughts: *This is awesome,* and *There's nothing like this in Philly!* A week later, Bobby and I began plotting what would eventually become Federal Donuts. *—TOM HENNEMAN*

DOUGHNUT VAULT

401 N FRANKLIN, CHICAGO, IL
DOUGHNUTVAULT.COM

UMMER OF 2013: MIKE AND I HAVE JUST FLOWN TO
CHICAGO TO COOK A DINNER AT A FUND-RAISER THAT
WOULD RAISE HUNDREDS OF THOUSANDS OF DOLLARS
TO FIGHT CHILDHOOD CANCER.

Events like these are a staple of the chef-driven restaurant world,
and we have the logistics down to a science. The day before the
event, we vacuum-sealed all the food we'd need and packed it in
dry ice in a disposable Styrofoam cooler. As we waited for it at
the baggage claim in Chicago, we said a little prayer for its safe
arrival. (There is always a chef at these events whose cooler doesn't

make it. This is followed by frantic tweets and texts asking if anyone in town can hook him or her up with some ground cherries or hemlock or sea anemones. Thankfully, the chef community is a resourceful and giving bunch.)

Our cooler finally emerged on the baggage claim belt, damaged but not destroyed, wrapped in packing tape in the style of the TSA or a three-year-old child. A chunk of Styrofoam was missing from the corner and a bag had leaked oil over everything, but the sea anemones were still alive.

It was too early to check into our hotel, so we ventured out into the wide streets of Chicago. It's an occupational hazard that any free moment we have in a different city is spent in search of food. So by the time we reached Doughnut Vault, we had already visited two other donut shops along the way. Which is to say, we weren't hungry.

Doughnut Vault was one of a handful of new-wave donut shops that had made it into the national consciousness, at least among the tiny minority that cares about such things. Occasionally, we were unfavorably compared to them on food blogs or Yelp. But I really didn't know anything about it: not what kind of donuts they were known for, or what the shop looked like, or who was behind it. For such a well-known spot, it seemed to have a low profile.

The place is tiny. You enter into the middle of a hallway (albeit a very cool hallway with vaulted ceilings covered in old brick, and tile walls). To your left is a short counter that runs the width of the space and separates you from the donuts. To your right is the end of the line, if it's not already snaking out the door. The whole thing is maybe a hundred square feet soaking wet.

All of us in this business are striving for a sort of authenticity, and we know that the more unassuming the place, the better the food. Doughnut Vault had an understated confidence that you could smell as the line crept forward. It smelled like donuts here!

Doughnut Vault's menu generally features only three donuts, with maybe a few kinds of glaze on top of that. But they tackle three totally different types. Perfecting just one of those styles is incredibly difficult, let alone all three. Their old-fashioned donut, rich with buttermilk, was fried gently for that characteristic exploded ring shape, as if tectonic plates of batter were pushing up against each other to create sweet, crunchy ridgelines. Next up, a perfect yeast-raised donut that didn't puff out its chest like other overproofed specimens to convince us that it was in a class by itself. And finally, the gingerbread stack, a trio of deep-flavored ringy cake donuts, the hardest of all donuts to nail, as tender at room temperature as a slice of birthday cake.

I'll stop short of saying in print that these were the best donuts I had ever had. After all, we are running a donut shop of our own. (But these were the best donuts I had ever had.) Oh, and also, $1 coffee. *—STEVEN COOK*

McMILLAN'S BAKERY

15 HADDON AVENUE, HADDON TOWNSHIP, NJ
(856) 854-3094

TO BECOME A CHEF, YOU MUST FIRST WORK FOR OTHER CHEFS, WHICH PUTS YOU IN A CONSTANT STATE OF SEEKING THEIR APPROVAL.

And no matter how successful you may become in your own right, you'll never stop wanting validation from those who taught you. And so it is with me and Marc Vetri, my friend and mentor. When we opened Federal Donuts, we got tons of praise from fans and critics alike, but to me, none of it mattered as much as what Marc thought. An early conversation went something like this:

ME: Hey, Cheffie, try this new fancy donut flavor—we call it "gunpowder green tea with overripe papaya and beef jerky." (We never served this donut.)

MARC VETRI: (Silence)

ME: Get it?! It's kind of like a Vietnamese papaya salad minus the fish sauce, but sweet!! So cool, right?

MARC VETRI: (Silence)

ME: Take a bite, bro!

MARC VETRI: (Silence, followed by tiny bite, followed by a wince.)

ME: What do you think?

MARC VETRI: Hey, man, have you been to McMillan's? Those donuts are really, really good!

I'd been hearing about McMillan's for years, from Marc but also from Brad Spence, a born-and-bred Jersey boy and Vetri's chef de cuisine (and now boxing manager), but I had never been there. One day, Steve and I decided to buy a cake for the Zahav staff meal to celebrate the restaurant's eighth birthday, and I suggested we use that as an excuse to check McMillan's out.

Located in a hamlet just across the Delaware River from Philadelphia, McMillan's is an old-school bakery that doesn't rely on hipsters, publicists, or gimmicks (like, say, *ahem,* fried chicken). Over more than seventy-five years, four generations of family members have taken their turn providing the community with its cream-filled needs. McMillan's predates the proliferation of the supermarket bakery counter, and I can't help but see Federal Donuts as part of a return to a world that prioritizes specialization and excellence over efficiency and convenience, values that were taken for granted when McMillan's opened its doors in 1939.

McMillan's is a full-service bakery, but their donuts in particular stand out. The humble cider donuts may not be much to look at, but to eat one is to go back in time to a world of unicorns and circus clowns and discover why donuts became a thing in the first place. The cream-filled donuts will rock your world. And their birthday cakes aren't half bad, either. *—MIKE SOLOMONOV*

McMillan's whipped cream–filled donuts will rock your world.

UNDERWEST DONUTS

638 WEST 47TH STREET, NEW YORK, NY
2 PENN PLAZA, NEW YORK, NY
UNDERWESTDONUTS.COM

ONE FALL DAY AFTER WALKING THE LENGTH OF THE HIGH LINE, I REMEMBERED HEARING ABOUT A NEW "CAKE" DONUT SHOP THAT HAD RECENTLY OPENED NEAR THE WEST SIDE HIGHWAY.

A few minutes later (thanks, Google), I arrived at my destination, which was, to my great amazement, a car wash. It takes audacity to open a donut shop in a car wash. I had arrived on foot, and with no dirty car; I was beginning to feel like an interloper. But then I found the tiny waiting room, where Brown Butter, Banana Milk, and Coconut Lime donuts shared floor space with Christmas tree–shaped air fresheners. These were far from the vending machine options you expect while waiting for your deluxe wash.

Owned by former Chanterelle sous chef Scott Levine and his wife, Orlee Winer, above (it's her father's car wash), Underwest is impossibly tiny. The customer side of the room is so narrow that

you literally have to belly up to the counter to let someone pass. The confines make the donuts all the more impressive. In comparison, Federal Donuts' 600-square-foot shops feel palatial.

After chasing a Maple Waffle and a Dark Chocolate donut with a cup of serious coffee, I wandered happily back into the streets of Manhattan. Underwest reintroduced me to the power of donuts. It had taken the idea of the waiting room—so loaded with negative connotations—and turned it on its head, investing it with entirely new and different meaning. At Underwest, the donuts transform their surroundings. Now, whenever I'm in New York, I make sure my car is just dirty enough for a wash. What can I say? I'm hungry. —*J. BRIEN MURPHY, FEDNUTS MANAGER*

181

STAN'S DONUTS

10948 WEYBURN AVENUE, WESTWOOD VILLAGE, CA
STANSDOUGHNUTS.COM

WHEN YOU WALK INTO STAN'S DONUTS, A LOS ANGELES INSTITUTION FOR MORE THAN FIFTY YEARS, ON A SATURDAY MORNING FOR THE FIRST TIME, YOU DON'T EXACTLY EXPECT TO SEE STAN.

And yet there he was, behind the counter of his iconic downtown Westwood Village corner shop, bagging donuts and schmoozing with customers. He seemed to know just about all of them. Stan Berman is in his eighties now. Back in 1964, his donut flavors may have raised eyebrows, but now the display case reads like classic donuts—only better. And Stan doesn't discriminate. He makes raised donuts, cake donuts, old-fashioned donuts, and assorted bars, fritters, rolls, logs, twists, and Danish. They are, perhaps, not the beautiful specimens we're accustomed to seeing on Instagram, but they taste that much better for it.

Stan has roots in Philadelphia, where his father and uncle ran bakeries, but he learned to bake in the Marines, who shipped him to Camp Pendleton in a move that could be considered the best thing to ever happen to West Coast Donuts.

As East Coasters, it's hard to think about Los Angeles as a donut town. Salad greens, sure, but movie stars don't eat donuts, right? (Actually, quite a few of them patronize Stan's.) But up close, Los Angeles is leagues deeper than it appears on-screen. And Stan's is the kind of old-school shop that reminds us of the universal appeal of donuts in the first place, attracting the construction worker, the UCLA student, and the guy in the bright-yellow Maserati in the No Parking zone out front.

It's exactly what we envisioned for Federal Donuts when we dreamt it up: a no-frills, bustling shop, long on over-the-counter banter and short on pretension. Thanks, Stan. *—STEVEN COOK*

GLAM DOLL DONUTS

2605 NICOLLET AVENUE S., MINNEAPOLIS, MN
GLAMDOLLDONUTS.COM

INK IS AN OBVIOUS DESIGN PRIORITY AT GLAM DOLL
DONUTS, THE GORGEOUS BRAINCHILD OF BUSINESS
PARTNERS TERESA FOX AND ARWYN BIRCH.

From the facade to the boxes to the coffee cup lids, Glam Doll is
awash in pink. Other recurring motifs include hearts and bacon. In
2013, the two Twin Cities donut queens left the corporate world to
join the artisanal donut revolution. Teresa, whose grandmother's
recipes are the basis of the shop's assortment of raised, filled, and
cake donuts, is the baker. Arwyn, a fashion designer, is in charge
of Glam Doll's retro-chic aesthetic. The partnership clearly works.
A second Glam Doll opened in Northeast Minneapolis in 2016.

The original shop is located on Eat Street, the mile-plus-long
stretch of Nicollet Avenue just south of downtown Minneapolis.
Over the last twenty years, several dozen ethnic, mom-and-pop,
and hipster restaurants, bars, and cafes have opened there, creating
eclectic and compelling destinations. After passing through the
pink storefront, customers meet a glass case filled with tray after

tray of brightly colored stuffed, sprinkled, and bedazzled donuts. A comfortable seating area wraps around the space—part punk rock, part '50s modern—offering a peek into the open kitchen, where the donuts are primped and styled for their fifteen minutes of fame (that's about how long they last before being devoured).

Glam Doll's logo is a pinup girl, but the donuts merit their own glamour shots. They're always well dressed, thankfully, avoiding

the arms race competition of who can pile the most stuff on top. And with names like Dark Angel (vanilla bean cream and chocolate), Femme Fatale (fresh raspberry curd and vanilla icing), and Pinup Girl (apple bourbon fritter—bacon optional), Teresa and Arwyn know how to optimize their titillating creations. But Glam Doll is not all about sin; the shop offers excellent vegan donuts, too. *—STEVEN COOK*

CURIOSITY DOUGHNUTS

19 BRIDGE STREET, STOCKTON, NJ
CURIOSITYDOUGHNUTS.COM

THERE COMES A POINT IN ALL CHEFS' CAREERS WHEN THEY REALIZE—DESPITE THE GRUELING TRAINING THEY'VE ENDURED, THE COUNTLESS BOOKS THEY'VE PORED OVER, AND ALL THE HOURS SPENT IN FRONT OF A STOVE—THAT THEY ACTUALLY DON'T KNOW A FUCKING THING ABOUT FOOD.

For me, that moment came in 2005, up in the attic "office" of Marigold Kitchen (my first executive chef job). My boss, Steven Cook, asked me if I had ever heard of the blog *Ideas in Food*. I lied. As soon as he left the room, I delved into the minds of Alex Talbot and Aki Kamozawa, and my mind was blown.

Turbot wrapped with passionfruit gel as a palate cleanser? Okay! Hot dogs as part of the raft for clarifying consommé? Sure! Chicken skin–wrapped tuna? So cool! (Pretty soon I was wrapping chicken skins around sweetbreads and declaring myself a genius.) The list goes on and on.

And now, after years of enlightening cooks with their blog and indispensable cookbooks, Alex and Aki have graced us with an amazing donut shop in a cute farmers' market less than an hour's drive from Philly. Their donuts are superlative—rich and inventive, handmade and luscious, in such flavors as Chocolate Yeasted Black and White, Buttermilk-Lime, and Apple Pie with Butterscotch Glaze.

Their frozen custard is out of control, and their fried chicken is pretzel-crusted and delicious. How lucky for us they don't serve coffee.
—MIKE SOLOMONOV

FIVE DAUGHTERS BAKERY

1101 CARUTHERS AVENUE, NASHVILLE, TN
BAKERY: 230 FRANKLIN ROAD, FRANKLIN, TN
FIVEDAUGHTERSBAKERY.COM

THERE'S NOTHING QUITE LIKE SEEING A CITY FOR THE FIRST TIME ON NO SLEEP AT THE END OF A GRUELING MONTH-LONG BOOK TOUR.

It happened to us in November 2015, when Steve and I boarded the red-eye from LA, missed our 4 a.m. connection in Chicago, and finally arrived at the last stop of our tour twelve hours later. That

was you, Nashville, and things were not looking so good for our future together. Jet-lagged and irritable, we nodded off in the back seat of a friend's car as he tried to show us the city. We'd heard Nashville had one of the most exciting emerging food scenes in the country, but we were in no shape to independently confirm that. We muddled through our cookbook event, and by the next morning, we'd recovered (I'm pretty sure I slept with my shoes on). And then we did what we always do: We went looking for donuts.

Five Daughters Bakery is a family business run by the husband-and-wife team of Isaac and Stephanie Meek. And yes, they have five daughters. How they manage that AND make such achingly beautiful and delicious donuts is outside the scope of this book. The main bakery is in Franklin, Tennessee, just south of Nashville, but we visited their shop in the 12 South neighborhood, a hip,

upscale enclave not too far from Music Row and Vanderbilt University. Just off the main commercial corridor, Five Daughters is located in a rehabbed Craftsman-style house with a sunny porch where you can enjoy your donuts in Nashville's hospitable climate.

Inside, the house is filled with light, the scent of buttery pastry, and the hum of happy people. Trays of donuts sit behind a glass case like precious jewels. As you point, a friendly counterperson fills your box, then you head back to the living room to pay the cashier. The donuts are vividly flavored and beautifully constructed. I was afraid I would smudge the Oreo glaze and ruin everything,

but I couldn't resist. Ditto for the Classic Strawberry and Chocolate Coffee Crunch. The base for most of Five Daughters' rotating flavor assortment is called the 100 Layer Donut, pictured above. A croissant-donut hybrid that takes more than three days to make, it took me like five seconds to eat.

And just like that, Nashville was looking a whole lot better. We had amazing food on that trip but it was the donuts at Five Daughters that changed things for us. A couple months later, we signed a deal to open our own donut shop in East Nashville (Five Daughters wouldn't hire us). *—MIKE SOLOMONOV*

BLUE STAR DONUTS

0672 № 2 SW GAINES STREET, PORTLAND, OR
AND MANY OTHER LOCATIONS
BLUESTARDONUTS.COM

I 'VE NEVER FELT MORE INSECURE IN THE DONUT BUSINESS THAN WHEN I SAW A COMPETITOR WITH THE TAGLINE "PORTLAND—TOKYO—LOS ANGELES."

To me, this meant that not only was Blue Star Donuts better than us, but smarter, too. At last count, this juggernaut has eight shops stateside (six in Portland, two in Southern California) and seven (!) in Japan. The first time I visited Blue Star, there was just one shop. I was in town for a food festival and meeting a former Zahav cook who'd moved to Portland several years earlier, when I had only the slightest inkling of the food nirvana that the city was or would become.

That original Blue Star is located on the edge of the Pearl District, a revitalized former warehouse neighborhood that runs north from downtown to the west bank of the Willamette River. It was a Saturday morning, and the first thing I noticed as we approached the shop was the line of customers already out the door and down the sidewalk.

Blue Star occupies an enviable corner storefront with full-length windows and double-height ceilings. An L-shaped blonde wood counter separates the customers from the bustling bakery. The owners, Katie Poppe (above) and Micah Camden, have opened dozens of restaurants together, but rather than feeling like part of a small corporation, Blue Star retains the earnest vibe of an independent bakery.

After we selected our donuts and paid, we shuffled to the end of the counter to wait for our donuts to be picked and packed. We watched a baker lift a large slab of dough onto a butcher-block table—dough that looked so supple and springy that I wished that I were their baker just so I could touch it.

Donuts are the quintessential everyman food, and flavors tend to skew lowbrow in the donut world (e.g., bacon, Fruity Pebbles). But at Blue Star, the donuts have gone full Portland. The raised donuts use brioche dough, which is like a regular yeasted dough that has swallowed several pounds of butter. The result is a dense and decadent donut that is lightened by the dough's eighteen-hour fermentation. Blue Star's patience is rewarded by donuts with a complex flavor that stands up to the gild-the-lily fillings, glazes, and garnishes.

High on that list are flavor combinations like Blueberry Bourbon Basil; Passion Fruit Cocoa Nib; and Blackberry Compote Peanut Butter Powder; flavors that take advantage of Portland's amazing produce and highlight its hip sensibilities. Blue Star's famous Cointreau Crème Brûlée donut is filled with rich vanilla custard and comes with a pipette of Cointreau Syrup that pierces the crunchy torched-sugar top for a very grown-up donut experience.

It's no wonder they're big in Japan. **—STEVEN COOK**

CHAPTER NINE

IT'S A FUNNY BUSINESS

DOUBLING DOWN ON CRAZY: THE ROOSTER SOUP STORY

ABOUT A YEAR AFTER WE OPENED OUR FIRST FEDNUTS STORE, THE FIVE OF US WERE CRAMMED IN A CAR ON THE WAY BACK FROM A MEETING. STORE NUMBER TWO WAS IN THE BAG, AND WE WERE PLOTTING THE NEXT STEP ON OUR MARCH TOWARD TOTAL WORLD DOMINATION.

One of us floated the idea that instead of building yet another store that was too small, we should consider a larger footprint that could double as a commissary to feed our growing empire. A commissary would ensure we would never again be publicly flogged for running out of chicken. For the first time, we would have the space to butcher whole chickens ourselves, improving freshness and quality control. And this, in turn, would allow us to use better, more environmentally friendly birds without raising prices.

EIGHTEEN MONTHS LATER, WE WERE UP TO OUR EYEBALLS IN CHICKEN PARTS (THANKS, LAW OF UNINTENDED CONSEQUENCES).

We're talking more than five hundred pounds of carcasses every week, the result of breaking down the chickens in our shiny new commissary. And those carcasses were going straight into the trash.

Enter Broad Street Ministry (BSM) and its Hospitality Collaborative. BSM itself was also a product of unintended consequences. Founding pastor Bill Golderer had come to Philadelphia in 2006 to breathe new life into a venerable but abandoned old church on Broad Street, one of the city's main arteries. He imagined a young, engaged congregation that could speak to the role of faith and community in the new millennium.

Mike (with Bill Golderer and Steve) wasn't chicken to try anything for fund-raising.

But when he began offering meals after Sunday services, he didn't get, as he'd expected, hipsters or young professionals or families with children as much as he got people who were vulnerable and suffering. And that is how BSM stumbled upon the concept of "Radical Hospitality."

THE PHRASE "HOSPITALITY BUSINESS" IS A CONTRADICTION. TRUE HOSPITALITY IS NOT TRANSACTIONAL.

It is a fundamental human interaction that comes with no strings attached. And yet there we were at Federal Donuts, earning our living by providing hospitality for money. Not that there's anything wrong with that, especially since we do it first for the love, and second for the money. Trust us, there are easier ways to make a buck.

When our company began volunteering at Broad Street Ministry in 2013, with our cooks and front-of-house staff alongside us, it was a gut check for us—an opportunity to practice what we preach in our professional lives every day. And it ultimately reaffirmed our faith in the power of hospitality. Today, BSM's Hospitality Collaborative serves more than seventy thousand meals a year. Guests are greeted by a host, seated at linen-covered tables, and served a three-course meal prepared by a professional chef and presented by an all-volunteer waitstaff.

Meals are only part of the story. BSM serves as a mailing address for more than three thousand Philadelphians, one that allows them to receive benefits, get a job, or find a place to live. And there are a dozen other social services available, ranging from a clothing closet to personal care packages to legal and medical assistance. But most important, there is the simple underlying idea behind Radical Hospitality: Everyone deserves to be invited to the table, and there is healing power in the invitation itself.

Broad Street Ministry is in the hospitality business—just at a different price point, a joke that Bill Golderer never misses an

Yememite Chicken Pot Pie at Rooster Soup.

Rooster soups (clockwise from top): Roasted Cauliflower, Smoked Matzo Ball, Mushroom Barley, and Beef & Vegetable.

opportunity to tell. But it's the truth, and this pure form of hospitality is what inspired us to collaborate with BSM on Rooster Soup. Which brings us back to chicken bones.

WHAT WOULD YOU DO—WHAT WOULD ANYONE DO—WHEN CONFRONTED WITH HUNDREDS OF POUNDS OF FREE HIGH-QUALITY CHICKEN BONES? YOU WOULD MAKE SOUP. OF COURSE YOU WOULD.

And the medium is the message. Restaurants as we know them started with roadside vendors selling soup to revive weary travelers. The word "restaurant" derives from the French "to restore." And that is the whole point of BSM's Radical Hospitality—to help people who have fallen through the safety net restore their dignity and humanity.

Our first idea was to deliver the soup to BSM to help feed their guests. But Broad Street isn't a soup kitchen—there are no lines, no ladles of slop. Delivering soup would only reinforce these negative stereotypes. Then we had a better idea. What if we made soup the anchor of a restaurant—a regular restaurant with one small difference: 100 percent of the profits would go to help fund Broad Street's Hospitality Collaborative. We would call it the Rooster Soup Company.

In the summer of 2014, we launched a crowd-funding campaign with the following premise: What if you could help someone who really needed it just by eating lunch? For all of its gleaming office towers, world-class educational and cultural institutions, and booming restaurant scene, Philadelphia is one of the poorest large cities in America. You can't walk a hundred yards without encountering someone who is suffering, but most of us have no idea what we can do to help. Some just want the problem removed from sight.

Rooster Soup Company opened in January 2017, a rebuttal to the notion that the city's business and nonprofit communities had irreconcilable differences on the issues of hunger and homelessness.

A meal is served at
Broad Street Ministry.

TWO AND A HALF YEARS EARLIER, MORE THAN 1,500 PEOPLE HAD BACKED OUR SUCCESSFUL CROWD-FUNDING CAMPAIGN, TELLING US WITH THEIR WALLETS THAT THE IDEA WASN'T SO CRAZY AFTER ALL.

Karma made us wait until the Year of the Rooster.

Run by our partner, chef Erin O'Shea, and general manager John Nicolo, Rooster is a classic luncheonette with a long counter and cozy booths, trimmed in vinyl, Formica, neon, and chrome. Rooster Soup Company serves breakfast, lunch, and dinner seven days a week; soups are the star (think Smoked Matzo Ball), and how about Erin's biscuit breakfast sandwiches, her patty melt, or her coconut cream pie (opposite)?

The restaurant is located steps away from the city's political, social, and economic centers, a deliberate decision to live in the middle of the conversation on how we deal with the intractable problems we face as a city. It's a place where people can make a tangible impact on their community. It's a place where food waste is converted into social action. It's a place to receive hospitality and a place to pass it on. And people are coming in droves, slurping down more than one thousand servings of soup each week and feeling good doing it.

Philadelphia has been good to Federal Donuts, and we wanted to leave the city a little bit better than we'd found it. Opening and running a nonprofit restaurant is the craziest thing we've ever done. And it feels great.

Bill's vision for Rooster Soup is no less ambitious than wanting people who visit Philadelphia to do three things:

1. SEE THE LIBERTY BELL
2. CLIMB THE ROCKY STEPS
3. EAT AT ROOSTER SOUP

But don't forget to try a donut. We still have to make a living.

8am - 8pm
Seven days

ROOSTER SOUP Co.

1526 SANSOM STREET PHILADELPHIA, PA 19102
ROOSTERSOUPCOMPANY.COM (215) 454-6939

SO WHAT ELSE IS NEW?

FEDERAL DONUTS MIAMI
250 NW 24TH STREET, MIAMI, FL

I N 2015, WHILE FRYING CHICKEN AT SOUTH BEACH WINE & FOOD FESTIVAL, WE TOOK A BREAK TO TOUR MIAMI'S WYNWOOD NEIGHBORHOOD. MAYBE IT WAS THE 80-DEGREE FEBRUARY WEATHER, OR THE BUZZ OF A CITY BURSTING WITH SO MUCH VITALITY, OR MAYBE IT WAS JUST THE STRAIGHT-UP ENTHUSIASM OF OUR FRIEND AND MIAMI REAL ESTATE BROKER SARA WOLFE, BUT WE WERE SMITTEN.

OUR FIRST MIAMI FEDNUTS (AND OUR FIRST OUTSIDE OF
PHILLY) OPENED IN MID-2017, IN THE HEART OF WYNWOOD.
WE COMMISSIONED A NOSEGO MURAL FROM THIS
CONCEPT SKETCH FOR THE INTERIOR. IT'S A TRIBUTE TO
THE FORMER WAREHOUSE DISTRICT'S SECOND LIFE
AS AN INTERNATIONAL (STREET) ART DESTINATION. AND
WE COULDN'T THINK OF A BETTER PLACE TO FANCY UP
SOME DONUTS.

HOLIER THAN THOU: DONUTS VS. BAGELS

TO THE UNTRAINED EYE, BAGELS AND DONUTS CAN SEEM VIRTUALLY IDENTICAL. TAKE, FOR EXAMPLE, THEIR COMMON CIRCULAR SHAPE, OR THE HOLE IN THE MIDDLE, OR THE WAY THEY'RE BOTH SOLD BY THE DOZEN. BUT BENEATH THESE SUPERFICIAL SIMILARITIES, DONUTS AND BAGELS ARE ACTUALLY QUITE DIFFERENT. TAKE IT FROM US—WE'RE DONUT EXPERTS. AND NOW, THANKS TO THIS HANDY GUIDE, YOU'LL NEVER AGAIN ORDER LOX AND CREAM CHEESE ON A CRULLER.

EAT DONUTS FOR HEALTH

Nutritionally speaking, both donuts and bagels are loaded with all the calories, carbohydrates, and gluten you need to carry you from one blood sugar peak to the next. But only donuts are loaded with refined sugar for those heroically higher highs and ludicrously lower lows.

ADVANTAGE: DONUTS

VARIETY IS THE SPICE OF LIFE

You could eat a different donut every day for a year and never repeat yourself. (In fact this is the subject of our next book: *A Donut a Day: The Unlikely Fountain of Youth*, A Rux Martin Book.) There are yeast donuts, cake donuts, and even potato donuts; crullers and old-fashioned donuts; long johns and fritters; plain donuts and donuts that are filled, glazed, sugared, and powdered. The list of fillings and toppings is infinite.

There are only four recognized bagels: sesame, poppy, onion, and pumpernickel. Everything bagels are a mere repackaging. Salt, egg, and whole wheat bagels are a minor footnote to the definitive scholarship. And now, to address the elephant in the room, cinnamon raisin: not a bagel. Ditto for blueberry and chocolate chip. And while we're at it, please stop with the strawberry cream cheese—that belongs on a donut.

ADVANTAGE: DONUTS

PERFECT FOR ANY OCCASION

To show our complete objectivity and absolute commitment to the truth, we will stipulate that bagels do make an ideal brunch. And bagels are the third biblical requirement for a bris (the others being a male Jewish baby and a sharp knife). But beyond that, we're hard-pressed to think of an occasion for which donuts are not the better option. Bagels on Fat Tuesday are weird and awkward. Likewise on National Donut Day. Donuts, on the other hand, are perfect for both. And donuts even make a spectacular alternative to a wedding cake (page 114). Marriages that are consummated with a bagel wedding cake end in divorce.

ADVANTAGE: DONUTS

In summary, while both bagels and donuts pair well with coffee, you know you want the donut.

TOP TWENTY REJECTED DONUT FLAVORS

1. OFFAL ÉCLAIR
2. GRASSHOPPER CRUNCH
3. OLIVE GARDEN
4. MAGIC MUSHROOM
5. CHERRY PEPTO
6. SWEET AND SOUR GRAPES
7. PEDIALYTE TROPICAL FRUIT
8. RED BULL AND VODKA
9. SCHUYLKILL RIVER PUNCH
10. ENSURE BRÛLÉE
11. HUMBLE BRAG PIE
12. DEVILED EGG
13. MEDICAL MARIJUANA
14. COFFEE BREATH
15. MARGARINE-PECAN
16. CRÈME DE MINT MOUTHWASH
17. FLAMING HOT NACHO CHEESE
18. MEAT LOVER'S
19. FETA-PAPAYA
20. BITTER MELON-CHOLY

HATE MAIL & NASTY REVIEWS: WISDOM FROM THE BLOGOSPHERE

LAUNCHING A BUSINESS, ALMOST ANY BUSINESS (BUT ESPECIALLY OUR BUSINESS), INTO THE CACOPHONY OF SOCIAL MEDIA ELICITS AN INEVITABLE AND ENDLESS STREAM OF COMMENTS. HEREIN, A RANDOM SAMPLE:

PART 1
THE CONCEPT IS FLAWED . . .

"And why doughnuts & chicken? Wouldn't a creative waffles & chicken joint have made more sense? Hell, serve the doughnuts if you want to, but there's got to be waffles . . . I'm sure the food's gonna be good, but it could have been so much more. Like crushing the ball into the gap for a triple when if you'd pulled it a little more it would have left the park."

"How do you go from Zahav to peddling this crap . . . downward spiral for Michael and Steven . . ."

"A regular coffee shop would probably be more viable in this neighborhood than a place with multiple banal gimmicks."

AND THE LOCATION SUCKS, TOO

"I'm interested, but what an awful out-of-the-way location . . ."

"This just proves my point that nobody is going to trek down to Pennsport, or whatever that area is, just for some donuts and chicken. If it was at, say, 19th and Chestnut, they would have been sold out of the donuts in 1 hour instead of 2, and out of the chicken within 10 minutes. 45 minutes? This place is going to fail within the week." [after opening day]

WE DON'T KNOW WHAT WE'RE DOING

"Dear hipster-chicken: I'm starting to think you don't actually have chicken but pay people to line up outside and talk about how awesome it is. If you do actually have chicken, you must be seeking clientele that have nothing better to do than wait outside for hours to get a ticket to get mediocre chicken. Then you can spend the rest of the afternoon drinking PBR."

"Yeah, actually, they called it quits after only one day. Mike Solo's already onto a new venture in Bridesburg called Universal Organs, featuring offal and éclairs."

"Same shit, different toilet."

"Let's make 83 donuts and sell out in an hour after we make people wait for donuts. I'm not really sure where this 'let's make a fake demand' for our donuts model came from, but it's annoying. If I owned a business and I were losing dozens and dozens of customers because I didn't make enough donuts— I would MAKE MORE DONUTS!"

"The hipsters may have time for this, but I sure don't."

PART 2
UNSOLICITED ADVICE (EMAIL EDITION)

NOTHING LASTS FOREVER

to: info@federaldonuts.com
subject line:
from: amy in Philadelphia

Really? You discontinued chocolate sea salt? Were you bored with it? Because we paying customers were not. I went to Federal Donuts in South Philly and Rittenhouse almost every weekend. If I went after 10 a.m., chocolate sea salt was always sold out. I wondered why on earth you would not just make more if you knew they were so popular. And now you take them off the menu? Removing an item that sells out does not seem too smart to me. I personally like the hot donuts, but my boyfriend only eats (ate) the chocolate sea salt. So, now we aren't customers anymore. (And no, he and I don't care for the chocolate malt—it is not a suitable replacement for a well-loved item.)

Hope you change your mind so I can start coming back to FD every weekend.

A LESSON IN CHICKEN ANATOMY

to: info@federaldonuts.com
subject line: white meat vs dark
from: drew in philly

Hi!

I was reading good things about Federal Donuts and so I checked out your menu online. Unfortunately, it seems that I have to buy both white meat and dark meat if I want to enjoy your food.

Let me explain: White meat and dark meat taste COMPLETELY DIFFERENT. There is no resemblance between the two, other

than they happen to come from the same animal. Some people love white meat and hate dark meat. Others (like me) love dark meat and hate white meat. And then there are some people who happen to love (or hate) both.

It is unconscionable that you would force your customers to buy both types of meat and not give us a choice. When you change your policy, then I will visit your establishment.

Thanks,
Drew in Philly

YE OLDE YELP BLACKMAIL

To: info@federaldonuts.com
From: █████████████████
Subject: Chicken was dry

On Sat nite we just ate the ½ buttermilk ranch chicken that I purchased at noon.
I asked the server before purchase if it could be reheated as dinner. He said "yes" and told me to put it in a 375° oven for 10 min. I followed his instructions.
Unfortunately, the chicken was extremely dry and somewhat tasteless. The coating was crispy.
I thought it came with cornbread but it came with a plain donut. The donut was tasty even when warmed. I had the donuts in the past and was eager to try the chicken.
I brought the meal home to surprise my partner. Unfortunately, it was a big disappointment. I tried calling the West Philly store, but it was already closed. I do not think that you should state that it can be reheated.
I will await your response before putting this review on Yelp.

THE FEDNUTS WORKOUT

RUNNING A DONUT SHOP IS HARD WORK. AT THE END OF THE DAY, WE'RE COVERED IN DONUT BATTER, CHICKEN FEATHERS, COFFEE GROUNDS, EGGSHELLS, FLOUR, CORNSTARCH, AND CANOLA OIL.

And in the fast-paced fried chicken business, it seems like there's never any time for the gym. So early on, we collaborated with Wade Hinnant, of the world-famous Joe Hand Boxing Gym, to develop a five-minute, anytime, anywhere workout using whatever we had on hand. The results were nothing short of amazing.

For most people, a diet of donuts and fried chicken would pack on the pounds. But no matter how much we ate, the FedNuts partners all lost weight while adding lean muscle mass. And now, for the first time, we're making this patented workout available to non–donut shop owners. We're so confident it will get you in the best shape of your life, we're willing to stake Wade's reputation on it!

For best results, follow our general manager Tommy Henneman's six positions exactly. Always work out with a partner for motivation and safety. And always use genuine FedNuts donuts and fried chicken parts.

FIG. 1 *SIDE PLANK*

Balance one dozen donuts in a box on the fingertips of your raised arm and hold a side plank position as shown. Have your partner say mean things about you. Repeat on the other side.

FIG. 2 *SQUATS*

With a chicken sandwich in each hand, extend your arms forward at shoulder height and squat until your hamstrings are parallel with the floor. Make sure your back remains straight so that the chicken sandwiches don't drip Spicy Rooster Sauce all over everything.

FIG. 3 *PUSHUPS*

Have your partner hold a "Fancy" donut right beneath your face so that you can take a bite on each downward movement. For beginners, do as many reps as it takes to eat one donut. As your stamina grows, increase to three donuts per set.

FIG. 4 *CRUNCHES*

Carefully cradle two dozen donuts on your shins and raise your torso to bring your elbows to your knees. Do five sets of thirty reps, eating a half dozen donuts after each set so that by the final set, there are no donuts left.

FIG. 5 **LEG RAISES**

Lift your legs over a stack of six Hot Fresh donuts while lying flat on your back with your head raised. Hold the position for as long as it takes to chug a cup of hot coffee.

FIG. 6 **PUSHUPS**

Have your partner sit on your lower back while you do pushups, then trade places. This is a good time for a mid-workout snack.

ACKNOWLEDGMENTS

THE PARTNERS OF FEDERAL DONUTS HAVE SO MANY PEOPLE TO THANK FOR MAKING THIS BOOK A REALITY.

To *RUX MARTIN*, for taking a chance on a book that at first may have seemed ridiculous, but eventually proved to be merely absurd. And for your wisdom and grace in making it the best version of itself.

To *DOROTHY KALINS*, for making something out of nothing, for herding cats, for your boundless talent, dedication, and friendship.

To *DON MORRIS*, for bringing life to the empty page and for being such a mensch.

To *MIKE PERSICO*, for your sharp eye, your tactical, photographic strike capabilities, and your cool vibes.

To *THE TEAM AT HMH*, especially *REBECCA LISS* and *BRAD PARSONS*, for working so hard to make us look good. It's a lot of work. Thanks, too, to *MELISSA LOTFY*, *JAMIE SELZER*, *JILL LAZER*, and *SARAH KWAK*, for your great eyes.

To *DAVID BLACK* and the *DAVID BLACK AGENCY*, for being in our corner and helping us sleep better at night.

To *MATT FEIN*, *BRIEN MURPHY*, *LAUREN CORREIA*, *MAX COHEN*, *JOSE RAMIREZ*, *LUIZ CANTOR*, and all the donut slingers and donut artisans past, present, and future—get back to work!

To *CHRISTIE ECHUCK* at bobbleheads.com, for your guidance and keen eye in the creation of our charming bobbleheads.

To *OUR CUSTOMERS*, you are the best customers a donut shop could ever dream of. Thank you in advance for standing by us, even after we sell out.

To *OUR PARTNERS*, colleagues, coworkers, business associates, distant relatives, and hangers-on, we couldn't do it without most of you. To *DANI MULLHOLLAND* for wrangling photos.

To *OUR FAMILIES*, for supporting us even before free donuts.

To *COFFEE*, for being so amazing; to *DONUTS*, for going so well with coffee; to *FRIED CHICKEN*, for being the best damn wild card ever.

IMAGE CREDITS

All photographs by **MICHAEL PERSICO** with the exception of the following:

Endpapers: Mural at Federal Donuts, 701 North 7th Street, Philadelphia, by **NOSEGO**

CAROL M. HIGHSMITH: America Collection Library of Congress: 13
ROGER SHERMAN: 14–15, 180, 181, 183, 199, 205
JESSICA KOURKOUNIS: 18, 34–35
Courtesy **FEDERAL DONUTS:** 25, 27, 29, 30, 114–115
MATTHEW FEIN: 33
SHARON ANCHEL: 170, 171
VINCE DOMINGUEZ: 172–173, 174, 175
THEO MORRIS: 184, 185
AKI KAMOZAWA: 186, 187
AUSTIN MARTIN: 194–195
TIM MOYER: 196–197
DAVID M. WARREN/PHILADELPHIA INQUIRER: Copyright © 2017, 202–203
NOSEGO: Sketch for Federal Donuts Miami mural, 206–207

FAN ART

CINDY CHAN: 117, cchansf@outlook.com
LORA MARIE DURR: 118–119, www.loramariedurr.com
BENJAMIN LONG: 120, www.benjaminlong.com
MIKE GENO: 121, www.mikegeno.com
PATRICIA BONGIORNO: 122–123, bongiornoillustration@email.com
ARIELLE MIRANDA GOLDBERG: 124, www.arielleg.com
JEREMY MILLINGTON: 125, jeremymillington@gmail.com
KELSEY RICE: 126, krice402@gmail.com
KARA BERGEY: 127, www.quirkycuriosities.com
LILY MEIER: 128, www.lilymeier.com
TIFFANY KHAW: 129, thk4037@gmail.com
TIM BARNES: 130, www.timbarnes.com
NINA MAKHIJA: 131
SYLVANA SAWIRES: 132, sylvana.sawires@gmail.com
SAM HENDERSON: 133, www.samtarver.deviantart.com
BRANDON MCNEELY: 134, brandesign82@gmail.com, www.liquifieddesign.com
ALLISON CHANG: 135, www.thebillowywave.com

INDEX

NOTE: PAGE REFERENCES IN *ITALICS* INDICATE PHOTOGRAPHS.

M

maple drizzle, 108, *109*
marshmallow
    glaze, 96
    lemon "meringue" with
        lemon glaze, 104, *105*
mascarpone glaze, 88, *88*
milk and coffee, *112*, 113
milk glaze, 78, *79*
milk glaze, basic, 74, *75*

N

Nutella drizzle, 92, *92*

O

oil, frying, 42

P

peanut butter
    chocolate glaze, 98, *98*
    drizzle, *98*, 99
pomegranate glaze, 92, *92*

R

rooster sauce, spicy, 163, *163*

S

sandwich, fried chicken, 162,
    163

sauce, spicy rooster, 163, *163*
sesame seeds
    pomegranate glaze, 92, *92*
    salted tehina glaze, 81, *81*
s'mores, *94–95*, 96
soy garlic glaze, 158
spice blends
    ballpark barbecue, 155, *155*
    buttermilk ranch, 154, *154*
    coconut curry, 153, *153*
    za'atar, 152, *152*
spicy rooster sauce, 163, *163*
strawberry
    glaze, 84, *87*
    lavender, 71, *71*
sugar mixes
    cinnamon brown sugar, 68,
        69
    strawberry lavender, 71, *71*
    vanilla spice, 64, *64*

T

tehina glaze, salted, 81, *81*

V

vanilla cream glaze, 84, *84*
vanilla spice, 64, *64*

Z

za'atar spice blend, 152, *152*